the
art of
success

the art of success

What No One Ever Taught You
(But You Still Need to Know)

JAMES MELOUNEY

THE ART OF SUCCESS

Published by Blue Cord Books

Copyright © 2016 by James Melouney

Edited by Michael J. Carr

Cover design by Emir Orucevic

Logo design by Polygenic Design Studio

All rights reserved

First Edition: May 2016

ISBN 978-0-9945058-0-4 (hardcover)

ISBN 978-0-9945058-1-1 (paperback)

ISBN 978-0-9945058-2-8 (e-book)

The National Library of Australia Cataloguing-in-Publication
data is available upon request.

For more information, contact James Melouney through
Twitter (@jmelouney) or e-mail (james@jamesmelouney.com),
or at www.jamesmelouney.com.

10 9 8 7 6 5 4 3 2 1

To those with the courage to live their dreams

Contents

Before We Begin

Here we sit, on this planet we call Earth, in this galaxy we call the Milky Way. We are a tiny speck, an incomprehensibly small dot in a vast and expanding universe.

We humans have long pondered the reason for our existence. *Why are we here?* It's a fascinating question—and one we may never have the answer to. But that's okay. The reality is that we *are* here, which leads us to an equally fascinating question: what are we going to do with the brief and fragile life we have been gifted with?

So we come to the purpose of this book: to share a philosophy that will guide you in creating and living the best life you can. For that is the ultimate success in life.

This philosophy is organized into eight parts: *the Foundation* and the *Seven Pillars* that it supports.

The Foundation: Accept Full Responsibility for Your Life

Pillar 1: Perceive the World to Your Advantage

Pillar 2: Always Strive for Growth

Pillar 3: Set Your Goals, Then Plan and Execute

Pillar 4: Understand "Success" and "Failure"

Pillar 5: Embrace Change and Take Risks

Pillar 6: Work Well with Others and Strive Toward Leadership

Pillar 7: See the Big Picture

While success is far from linear—it has no ABC formula—these parts have been ordered deliberately.

As we take this journey, it won't be just you and me. Others—134, to be precise—will be coming along with us. For this book is built on the wisdom of some of history's greatest exemplars. You will learn from billionaires and business gurus; sports stars and rock stars; philosophers, emperors, inventors, and saints.

Such diversity of thought is vitally important, for although we humans are similar in many ways, we are also unique. And therefore, we need a variety of ideas to help us develop our own philosophy.

The messages and teachings of these exemplars are spread throughout the book. Each chapter contains an introductory overview, subheadings that group quotes from our exemplars, a discussion on each quote, and concluding remarks.

This design retains each exemplar's original voice and message, which you can mine for whatever wisdom speaks to you. It also attempts to deal with the inherent limitations of quotes: great wisdom condensed into few words, with little context—and context is key to understanding.

To the exemplars, my deepest thanks. Your words have inspired me, and it is my hope that through this book, your words will continue to inspire others.

And with that, we begin.

Accept Full Responsibility for Your Life

No One Else to Blame

Design Your Life

Find Your Path

Start with the Basics

SUCCESS IN LIFE is less about what happens to us than about how we respond to what happens. This is because we often cannot control what life throws at us, but we can control what we do with it.

Thus, the first step toward success is to accept full responsibility for our lives—to take ownership of all we think, say, do, and feel. To recognize that every one of our goals, dreams, desires, and ambitions is entirely up to us.

That's right. Success is on *us*. Of course, we are free to blame others for the situation we find ourselves in, but to what benefit? Even if the blame is justified, it still leaves us stuck where we are.

Once we are ready to stop blaming others, we must then actively design our life and find our path. Health, fitness, intimacy, or financial prosperity doesn't just happen by itself. We must *cultivate* these in our life. And we must also search for—and then take—the path that's right for us.

No matter your age, circumstances, or history, you have the opportunity to take control of your life: to accept full responsibility for where you are today, where you want to be tomorrow, and how you will get there. After all, it's your life, isn't it?

No One Else to Blame

If you are not in the process of becoming the person you want to be, you are automatically engaged in becoming the person you don't want to be.

—Dale Carnegie

Where you are today is a result of two things: the circumstances of your birth, and the sum of all your decisions up to now. Like all of us, you had no say in where and when you arrived into this world, and you've probably made some good decisions and some bad decisions. That's fine, because you can't change your past.

What's important is to realize that from this moment onward, every decision you make, action you take, thought you think, word you speak, and emotion you feel moves you either toward the life you desire, or in some other direction. To acknowledge this is the beginning of accepting full responsibility for your life.

You can't change your destination overnight, but you can change your direction—if you choose to.

The final forming of a person's character lies in their own hands.

—Anne Frank

Success is not about what you get; it's about what you *become:* the philosophy you cultivate, the skills you learn, the values you embody, the character you develop. And who you become has less to do with your circumstances than with your decisions.

In life, we all must face unexpected obstacles, experience disappointing setbacks, and know the bitter taste of defeat. That much is certain. What is less certain is how we will react. Will we blame others, or take responsibility ourselves?

Those two options represent a fork in the road. One road leads onward, toward all that you could ever want. That road is called *Responsibility*. And the other loops back on itself, leaving you stuck in the very same spot. It is the road named *Blame*.

It can be a terrifying thing, accepting full responsibility for our life. At that point, we grasp that we have no one but ourselves to blame. The good news is, once the panic subsides, liberation begins.

> *Everyone thinks of changing the world, but no one thinks of changing himself.*
>
> **—Leo Tolstoy**

Many of us yearn to have an impact, to become someone important, influential, respected. Yet what do we do about it? Often, not much. We continue working the same job, eating the same food, thinking the same thoughts. And then we blame our lack of success on anything but ourselves.

One of the biggest differences between those who stumble along through life and those who live out their dreams is *blame*. Laying the blame outside yourself leaves you powerless against the circumstances of life. You are left to the whims of the universe.

Don't cede power over your life to forces outside your control. Instead, choose to accept that your problems and their solutions, your failures and your success, lie first and foremost with you, not with others.

> *You may see at one and the same time both your best friend and your greatest enemy, by stepping in front of a mirror.*
>
> **—Napoleon Hill**

Your greatest hindrance and your greatest friend sleeps in your bed every night. No, I'm not talking about your spouse. I mean *you*.

You are the one who can hinder your success, and you are also the one who can accelerate it. And the key to accelerating your success is found in understanding yourself.

Start exploring who you are. Start understanding your weaknesses and temptations so you can mitigate their risks. Start identifying your strengths and passions so you can leverage your best assets. And start silencing your inner critic while amplifying your inner advocate, so you don't become your own obstacle.

By blaming others, you waste a precious opportunity to understand yourself better, which means you also lose out on the opportunity to move toward mastering yourself. And when you master yourself, success is close at hand.

Stop the blame. Master yourself. *Then* take on the world.

> **Seeing yourself as a victim is completely self-defeating . . . It's an attitude that kills all your options.**
>
> **—Jack Welch**

We all will face trials in life—some of us more than others, but no one is spared. That's why it is fruitless to dwell on the unfortunate events that have occurred in your life. Far better to ask: what am I going to do about it?

Unfortunately, most people tend to see themselves as victims of circumstance—of an industry in decline, a terrible manager, or an abusive relationship—rather than as the masters of their own destiny.

To be clear, some situations in life are terrible, but we only make a bad situation worse when we see ourselves as the victim, because in that moment, we relinquish our power to change it.

Whatever the situation—whether directly or indirectly caused by you, or from causes entirely beyond your control—blaming others is not only a waste of energy; it is also an inhibitor of the change you desire.

> *We are taught you must blame your father, your sisters, your brothers, the school, the teacher—you can blame anyone, but never blame yourself. It's never your fault. But it is always your fault, because if you wanted to change, you're the one who has got to change. It's as simple as that, isn't it?*
>
> **—Katharine Hepburn**

You are free to blame anyone or anything. You can blame your parents, your friends, the company you work for, the economy, the government, the weather—the list is a long one. But the reality is, in your life, the buck stops with you.

Poor health? That's on you. Empty bank account? That's on you. Disharmonious relationships? That's on you. It's *all* on you—and that's beautiful.

Your life is under your control. You can push yourself to your limits, take your abilities to their full, amazing capacity, and live the life of your dreams—but only when you accept that your life is completely, entirely, and indisputably your responsibility.

If you're stuck blaming others, you can be no more than a spectator in life. Isn't it time to get in the game?

Design Your Life

"My dear fellow, who will let you?"
"That's not the point. The point is, who will stop me?"

—The Dean and Howard Roark
(in *The Fountainhead*)

The world is an amazing place. It is chock-full of opportunity, but also of challenge. After all, if it were easy, succeeding wouldn't mean much.

As you venture forth, keep this in mind: you can and you must design the life you want. Whether the arena is health, relationships, spirituality, financial prosperity, or something else, it is up to you to determine where you want to go, and then take yourself there.

This is true even amid all the unfairness and inequality that exists in the world. It doesn't matter where you find yourself today; there is a way to guide yourself out of the darkness and into the light.

Oprah Winfrey found the path. She overcame poverty and sexual abuse to become a household name all around the world. So did Howard Schultz. He went from living in a Brooklyn housing project to becoming the CEO of Starbucks, and a billionaire.

How did they do it? They accepted full responsibility for designing the life they desired. For arranging every piece of the puzzle that needed to fall into place before their dreams could come true.

Only you can decide the kind of life you want to live. And only you can make that a reality.

I am the master of my fate,

I am the captain of my soul.

—William Henley

Are you the master of your fate, the designer of your future? Or are you not quite sure where you're headed? In life, each of us is the captain of our own ship. We must decide what we want, chart a course for it, and go.

Naturally, some people are blessed with more favorable conditions than others. Some people are born into a loving family, in a safe country with a free democracy. Not everyone is so lucky.

But regardless of your lottery ticket at birth, the rules of success still apply: if you want to change your life, you have got to do what your circumstances require.

That is the essence of designing your life. First, consider where you are today. Second, look to the horizon and determine where you want to go. And third, with those two places in mind, create a plan to get from A to B.

We create the life of our dreams. We claw our way out of darkness. There is no other way.

Those who simply wait for good things to happen really would be lucky to encounter them.

—Ken Robinson

Many people take a highly reactive approach to life. They are always *waiting*. They are waiting for the right job to present itself, the love of their life to magically appear, or their net worth to grow on its own. It is the equivalent of setting yourself adrift in the open ocean, without a sail or rudder, and hoping to find habitable land.

Don't leave your life to chance. Accept the mission to draw together all the necessary ingredients and create the life you dream of.

If you don't design your life—if you simply wait for good things to come to you—who knows what you'll end up with?

> *Dare to live the life you have dreamed for yourself. Go forward and make your dreams come true.*
>
> **—Ralph Waldo Emerson**

Few people have the courage to design their life and then live their dreams—to identify what they truly desire, create a plan to get it, and then take whatever action is necessary. That's because accepting full responsibility for our lives is a big mental leap from the way most of us are educated.

Still, there is no excuse for getting up every day, slogging through the same dreary tasks, and doing nothing to change it all. Change will come; it always does. But will that change move you forward, or backward? Will it take you where you want to go, or somewhere else?

If you want tomorrow to look different—and better—start designing it today. You won't stumble onto the life of your dreams; that's a guarantee.

Find Your Path

Let's assume that you think you have a choice of eight paths to follow (all predefined paths, of course). And let's assume that you can't see any real purpose in any of the eight. Then—and here is the essence of all I've said—you must find a ninth path.

—Hunter S. Thompson

One of life's greatest challenges is to live true to ourselves. To recognize our unique desires, goals, and ambitions. To find the overlap between what we're passionate about, what we're good at, and what we value. To walk *our* path in life.

What do you want to do with the precious few years you have on this planet? What kind of life does your soul call for? What sort of legacy will you weave into the fabric of time?

Too often in life, people entrust their dreams to others. They surrender these precious gifts to their friends, family, or the norms of society. And then they end up living a life they never truly wanted.

For better or worse, you are the one who must live with the consequences of your actions. If you need to, don't hesitate. Find that ninth path. (The remaining pillars reveal how.)

One of the greatest things you have in life is that no one has the authority to tell you what you want to be. You're the one who'll decide what you want to be.

—Jaime Escalante

We are influenced by our friends, family, and society. There's no denying it. Sometimes the message is so subtle, we may not even notice it nudging us in a particular direction. Other times, it's obvious, such as when our parents weigh in on where we should live, or when our kids lobby for the kind of car we should buy.

Even though it may not seem so right now, life is fragile and short. Don't waste it walking a path that's not right for you. Don't waste your time on things you don't find meaningful. And stop trying to please everyone—it's impossible.

Your life is one among billions. Does that make it insignificant? No. It's *your* life. It's *all* you've got. So find the path that's right for you, then walk it.

> *It seems implausible that our society could be gravely mistaken in its beliefs and at the same time that we would be alone in noticing the fact. We stifle our doubts and follow the flock because we cannot conceive of ourselves as pioneers of hitherto unknown, difficult truths.*
>
> **—Alain de Botton**

It's easy to be swept up in the consensus of the masses and absorb popular beliefs as our own. But the popularity of a thought does not mean it is right for you.

Part of finding your path involves examining your thoughts and beliefs, to determine whether these are (1) sound, (2) your own, and (3) what you truly desire.

Do you want to work a nine-to-five job? Do you want to get married and have children? Do you want a big house (with a big mortgage)?

It may seem pointless to question so-called common sense, but we must judge an idea by the soundness of its logic as it relates to *our* desires, not by how popular or fashionable it is.

The most contrarian thing of all is . . . to think for yourself.

—Peter Thiel

In a world that is constantly connected, getting even one hour to be alone with our thoughts is a great challenge. But without a little isolation, it is difficult to think independently.

When looking for your path, give yourself some space from society. Shut out the rest of the world for just a little while. You don't need to spend hours alone. Ten minutes entirely to yourself each day can do wonders.

If you neglect this, that inner voice trying to reach you may never get through all the noise going on around you. And you may find yourself, a decade from now, frustrated and stuck in yet another traffic jam instead of cruising down the road you're meant to be on.

When we all think alike, we're probably not thinking all that much. And our thoughts are not likely our own. Break free from the herd mentality that exists in every society. Spend some time with *you*.

Start with the Basics

If you correct your mind, the rest of your life will fall into place.

—Lao Tzu

Your mind determines the thoughts you have. The thoughts you have determine the actions you take. And the actions you take determine the life you live.

The trouble is, the mind is a *battleground*. War is waged there every day, and success is possible only for those who win the fight and take control.

Who's fighting? The enemy is complacency, jealousy, envy, fear, neglect, timidity—all those gremlins that live in our minds. And on our side, in the commander's seat, is our *philosophy*—the way that we think about ourselves, others, and the world.

To win the war that rages in your mind, start refining your philosophy. *Read* the great books. *Observe* yourself and others. *Digest* the wisdom you come across. *Question* what you find. And *apply* what you deem worthy.

The information you put into your mind, and the thoughts you allow to flourish there, are every bit as important as the food you put into your body.

Get your mind right, and the rest will follow.

In reading the lives of great men, I found that the first victory they won was over themselves . . . Self-discipline with all of them came first.

—Harry S. Truman

Self-discipline is one of the most important ingredients of success. It is more vital than any skill or habit. It supersedes goal setting, time management, and leadership.

Only with self-discipline can we direct ourselves to learn the skills that will enable us to turn our dreams into reality—skills such as how to set goals, how to be productive with our time, and how to lead others. And only with self-discipline can we consistently apply all that we have learned.

If life were a kitchen, self-discipline would be the cook: the one responsible for gathering the necessary ingredients, following the correct recipe, using the right cookware, and making the meal. In other words, the one responsible for making the most of all that is available.

If you are seeking success, start cultivating your self-discipline. There are no shortcuts.

If we have any lack, it is not because we lack money or opportunity or resources; it is because we lack ideas.

—Jim Rohn

As we begin accepting full responsibility for our lives, it is important to identify the root cause of our problems. Often, what we believe to be a problem is not the actual problem, but merely a *symptom* of the problem.

Poor health? That's usually not the problem. Lack of financial prosperity? That's not a problem. The real problem is lack of information and ideas that enable us, for example, to adopt a healthy lifestyle or create financial independence. This is why learning why and how to study is critical to your success.

Here's the formula: (1) What information do you need? (2) Where can you find it? (3) What are you waiting for? Go get it.

There is little difference between someone who can't read and someone who can yet chooses not to.

> *Motivation is a fire from within. If someone else tries to light that fire under you, chances are it will burn very briefly.*
>
> **—Stephen R. Covey**

Two traits can distinguish you from almost everyone else on Earth, and all but guarantee success. The first is a relentless drive to improve yourself and the world around you—a manifesto to get up every day determined to make the world better.

The second is unwavering courage in the face of failure—fearlessness of being wrong or coming up short. Then, when you fall down, you get up and begin again. No matter what.

The issue is, we can acquire these traits only if we are motivated, and motivation doesn't just magically happen by itself.

Reasons are what drive us in life. They are why we get up early, stay up late, and keep going no matter how tough it is. If you don't have your "why"—the *reasons* you do what you do—it is little wonder you aren't motivated.

It is your responsibility to examine your deepest desires and identify your "why." The motivation to succeed will follow.

> *There are three wicks, you know, to the lamp of a man's life: brain, blood, and breath. Press the brain a little, its light goes out, followed by both the others. Stop the heart a minute and out go all three of the wicks. Choke the air out of the lungs, and presently the fluid ceases to supply the other centers of flame, and all is soon stagnation, cold, and darkness.*
>
> **—Oliver Wendell Holmes**

The link between mind and success is clear to most people. What's less clear is the importance of the *body*.

Think of your body as the execution mechanism for your mind. It's what takes your dreams and goals and plans and turns them into reality.

If you're tired all the time, can't drag yourself out of bed in the morning, or can't make it up two flights of stairs without panting, life is going to be much harder than it needs to be.

Be wise enough to develop and maintain a healthy body. Take the time to study nutrition and fitness, and then apply what you learn. Your body is the only one you're going to get. Treat it as if you wanted it to last.

> *Take criticism seriously, but not personally. If there is truth or merit in the criticism, try to learn from it. Otherwise, let it roll right off you. Easier said than done.*
>
> **—Hillary Clinton**

Criticism is inescapable in life. But the advice we get from others won't always be right for us. That's because each of us is shaped by our own unique experiences, and so, despite our best efforts, our messages tend to be biased.

The challenge is twofold: First, learn to identify which advice is worth keeping and which to (graciously) ignore. Listen carefully to those who have what you desire. Listen cautiously to those who do not. And second, always value undue criticism over unwarranted praise. For even though undue criticism may hurt, unwarranted praise can debilitate and destroy.

Far better to be saved by criticism than ruined by praise. But remember, not everything you hear is worth listening to.

We find comfort among those who agree with us—growth among those who don't.

—Frank A. Clark

Who do you spend your time with? What do they have you reading? What do they have you thinking? Who do they have you *becoming*?

Each of us should reflect on the sort of people we have in our lives. While this can seem elitist, be under no illusions: you are, in part, the product of the people you spend most of your time with. This means you are likely to be about as successful as they are. And they either hamper or accelerate your success.

Seek out people and environments that will challenge and stimulate you, that will get you to think differently about yourself and the world. Seek out people and environments that will lead you toward the type of person you wish to become, and the life you wish to create. And distance yourself from people and environments that do not.

It will be painful, but these are some of the hard calls that successful people have to make. And if you won't make the call, then who will?

And so . . .

Accepting full responsibility for our lives is a process that happens differently for each of us. For some, it's a slow and steady affair. For others, it's a sudden and unexpected epiphany. And sadly, for too many, it never happens.

The inescapable truth is that whether you become the person you are capable of becoming, and live the life you are capable of living, is entirely up to you.

You have a choice. You can walk the well-trodden path of mediocrity and complacency and go right on blaming others for what happens (or doesn't happen) in your life. Or you can accept full responsibility for designing your life, finding your path, and turning your dreams into reality.

It's both a blessing and a curse: we are blessed with the opportunity to live the life of our dreams, and cursed with the choice to do it or not.

Responsibility for your life has been, and will always be, yours alone.

Perceive the World to Your Advantage

Change Your Mind, Change Your Life

It's All in How You Look at It

Perception Creates Reality

Why Not You?

The Beauty of Life

A CORE CONTRIBUTOR to success is the ability to perceive ourselves and the world to our *advantage*. The first step toward harnessing this power is to become aware that many times each day, each of us makes a choice—whether consciously or unconsciously—of how we perceive the world.

We can choose to perceive ourselves through a lens of socially imposed or self-imposed limitations. Or we can broaden our perception of what is possible for us to achieve, realizing that the only barriers are those we agree to accept.

We can choose to perceive the world as a hostile battleground, full of problems and traps and failure and excuses, or we can choose to perceive a challenging but fair learning environment, with an abundance of opportunity wherever we look.

And we can choose to perceive the world as a mundane, unchanging reality—the same old thing every day—or we can choose to see the radiant color, hear the vibrant sounds, and feel the contagious joy bursting forth from every moment.

The most successful people are those who have learned how to perceive the world to their advantage. And so must you, if you want to create the best life you can.

Change Your Mind, Change Your Life

A new type of thinking is essential if mankind is to survive and move toward higher levels.

—Albert Einstein

Einstein alludes to the fact that the world today is a result of our collective thinking. And because we created it by our thinking, to change it we must change the way we think. The same is true in your life. The life you lead is a direct result of both *how* you think and *what* you think about.

A new car doesn't make a new man. A Gucci dress does not create a lady. And a grand house does not draw a family closer together. It is our *thinking* that defines us. The kind of life we live is directly related to the thoughts we have.

For our thoughts determine our actions, our actions shape our habits, our habits form our character, and our character determines our existence. Through our thinking, we are the architects of our lives—and some of us are drawing in the dark.

To have what you've never had, go where you've never gone, and do what you've never done—to change your life for the better—*change your thoughts*.

But what will man do? He wants to be great, and he sees himself small. He wants to be happy, and he sees himself miserable. He wants to be perfect, and he sees himself full of imperfections.

—Blaise Pascal

When Albert Einstein was working at the Swiss patent office, did he know he would uncover some of the universe's greatest secrets?

And when Bill Gates failed with one of his earliest business ventures, Traf-O-Data, was he aware that he would one day become the world's richest man? Probably not. What does that mean? It means that who we are today is a mere fraction of who we can become. But it isn't always easy to see the possibilities.

To better comprehend the potential of the future, we must try to broaden the naturally limited view that we hold of the world and of ourselves.

Don't see the world as the city, state, or country you live in. It's a far bigger arena than that. Don't limit the world to the profession, company, or industry you work in—it is far broader. And don't downsize the world based on where you have been and what you have accomplished so far—the possibilities for the future are vastly greater.

You can do and become far more than you think, but only if you broaden your perspective on life, the world, and yourself. Only if you change your mind.

The greatest discovery of all time is that a person can change his future by merely changing his attitude.

—Oprah Winfrey

Your attitude toward life determines not only how you interact with others. It also governs how you interact with yourself. That is, your attitude influences *every* aspect of your life, which is why it's so important to get right.

But how are attitudes formed? Our attitude is shaped largely by the way that we perceive the world, for attitude ultimately reflects perception. Perceive a world of opportunity and abundance, and your attitude will reflect this. Perceive a world of misfortune and scarcity, and your attitude will reflect that, too.

Attitude can enable success or predispose us to failure—it can change lives. If you want a better attitude, try perceiving the world to your advantage.

Whatever a monk keeps pursuing with his think-ing and pondering, that becomes the inclination of his awareness.

—Siddhártha Gautama, the Buddha

Thoughts can destroy our self-confidence or lead us to create great business empires. Thoughts can paralyze us with fear or liberate us from that very same fear. And thoughts can shackle us in place or enable us to grow into our highest possible self.

The important thing, as the Buddha said, is to realize that what we focus on is what inevitably ends up in our life. This is why we must focus on what we *want*—every day.

Don't let a single day go by when you're not thinking about your goals and your dreams, and reminding yourself that you are worthy of success. The future is far more malleable than you probably believe it to be, but to shape it, you have to change the way you think.

I'm all in favor of keeping dangerous weapons out of the hands of fools. Let's start with typewriters.

—David Gerrold

Ideas are powerful. Not only are they powerful—they can be downright *dangerous*. Why? Because ideas transform lives, both for better and for worse.

Ideas can hobble us with the perception that success is unat-tainable no matter what we do. Ideas can lead us to believe that we cannot design our future, placing us at the mercy of our circumstances. And ideas can steer us so far off course that it's all but impossible to get back on track.

But ideas can also inspire us to develop new skills and follow our intuition. Ideas can explain to us the secrets behind the functioning of our minds and the complexities of our emotions. And ideas can shed light on the way the world "works," thereby enabling us to take advantage of all the opportunity that comes our way.

Always be vigilant with the ideas you are consuming—even the ones in this book. For when you change your mind, your life will change.

It's All in How You Look at It

Catching polio opened many more doors for me than the one it so firmly closed at the time.

—Ken Robinson

Ken Robinson contracted polio at age four. Many years later, reflecting on his life, he spoke the words above. While this is an astounding statement, and a testament to overcoming adversity, it is unlikely that he felt this way when he first comprehended the news of his diagnosis. This represents the sometimes crucial difference between what is *possible* to perceive and what we can perceive in the moment.

Right now, you may think you're stuck. After doing your job, raising your children, and paying the bills, you're out of both time and money. What can you do? You don't see any way out. But there *is* a way out, because the world is far greater than you perceive it to be.

Indeed, the opportunities are far more abundant, and the constraints far less limiting, than we tend to realize. But before we can take advantage of all that is out there, we must refine the way we look at life.

Try taking a fresh look at your life. Start questioning things you have always assumed to be true or unchangeable. The human mind has a tendency toward self-deception, but just as we can blindfold ourselves, within an instant our mind can reveal to us an unfamiliar world.

Is a man what he seems to the astronomer, a tiny lump of impure carbon and water crawling impotently on a small and unimportant planet? Or is he what he appears to Hamlet? Is he perhaps both at once?

—Bertrand Russell

The way you perceive the world can elevate you and boost your confidence, or drag you down and drown you in doubt.

Do you see yourself as an insignificant lump of carbon, or as a member of the most advanced species in the known universe? Both perspectives are valid, but the outcomes from adopting one versus the other are vastly different.

The first perception may lead you toward a life of fear and apprehension, a life in which you are reticent, unassertive, inhibited, and constantly nervous. The second perception could lead to a life full of self-confidence, conviction, boldness, and courage—a life in which you find out what truly matters to you, and go after it with all your heart.

There is enormous potential within you, waiting to be unleashed. But that can happen only when you can see this for yourself.

You can complain because rose bushes have thorns, or rejoice that thorn bushes have roses.

—J. Kenfield Morley

Isn't it interesting how two people can perceive the same situation in completely different ways? Some see opportunity where others see only challenge. Some see growth where others see only discomfort. And some see the possibilities of the future while others see only the messy, problematic present.

You know people of each mind-set: those who say, "I could never do that," and the ones who say, "Why not give it a try?"

Which group are you in? The way you look at life is your choice.

There is nothing either good or bad, but thinking makes it so.

—William Shakespeare

Your mind can transform any situation into a positive, growth-oriented experience that helps you on your journey. It's what successful people do: no matter the situation, they find opportunity in adversity, use discomfort to grow, and learn from failure. As a result, they approach life's events with a positive frame of mind and a powerful expectation of success. Unfortunately, most of us don't do this. But we can—if we train ourselves to.

Is the unexpected work assignment from your boss just a hassle, or a great opportunity to demonstrate your skills and get noticed?

Is the tattoo you got at 3 a.m. in Tijuana just an embarrassment, or a lesson that will serve you (and your kids) in the future?

Does getting old spell the end of adventure, excitement, pleasure, and joy, or signify the beginning of a different set of experiences—from which you can still find excitement and adventure, joy and pleasure?

This is not rocket science. Learn to see obstacles as opportunities, failures as learning experiences, and every dark cloud as mere camouflage for the silver lining hidden within.

> *Everything that happens in our lives—every misfortune, every slight, every loss, and also every joy, every surprise, every happy accident—is a teacher, and life is a giant classroom.*
>
> **—Arianna Huffington**

Our lives are no more than the accumulation of many different experiences. Naturally, some experiences are more fun than others, but every one of them can impart a lesson. It doesn't matter if it's a heartbreaking divorce, an unexpected layoff, or a humiliating joke that we are the butt of—there is always something to learn from it.

To perceive the world in this way is to perceive the world with a growth-oriented mind-set—and that's a powerful mind-set to have. With it, you can approach obstacles with confidence, knowing that you can transform failure into learning. And it prompts you to search for the silver lining that hides in every situation, leading you to discover value in places most people would not. Simply put: it is a mind-set that leads to success.

There is always opportunity in adversity, growth in challenge, and a glimmer of light in the darkness. Sometimes, you just have to look a little harder to find it.

You may not realize it when it happens, but a kick in the teeth may be the best thing in the world for you.

—Walt Disney

Did you know that Walt Disney was once fired for a lack of imagination and good ideas? That Steven Spielberg was rejected from the University of Southern California's film school? Or that J. K. Rowling faced eight publisher rejections before Bloomsbury picked up her first Harry Potter novel? And yet, they all went on to accomplish extraordinary things. Why?

The answer boils down to two reasons. First, despite rejection, they continued to believe that success was possible for them. And second, they found value even in the least promising circumstances, when their egos were bruised, their confidence shattered, and the will to succeed taxed to its limit.

When life knocks you around, look for the lesson. And never let go of the belief that you are capable of achieving your dreams.

The impact that the events *in* your life have *on* your life ultimately depends on how you look at those events.

Perception Creates Reality

> *We will act consistently with our view of who we truly*
> *are, whether that view is accurate or not.*
>
> **—Tony Robbins**

Your beliefs about who you are, what you deserve, and what you are capable of determine how you act in the world—and, in turn, determine how the world responds to you. But keep in mind that beliefs are based on *perception*.

If we perceive the world as full of opportunity and people who want to help us, we are more likely to believe that we are capable and deserving of success. And so that is how we act, and the world has no choice but to respond.

On the other hand, if we perceive the world as a hostile environment, where people are out to get us and where catastrophic risks lurk behind every corner, then we're more likely to see success as out of reach for us. And as we believe, so it becomes.

Before you can achieve success, you need to believe you're capable of achieving it. And that is far easier when the world you see is on *your* side.

> *We temper our ambitions based on the feedback we*
> *receive from others. Are you an extrovert or an intro-*
> *vert? Do you rely on intuition or rational thinking to*
> *make decisions? The unfortunate reality is that what*
> *holds most people back is actually their own beliefs*
> *that they are not good enough or deserving enough to*
> *be successful.*
>
> **—Jay Samit**

We act in alignment with what we believe. This is why we seldom become more than we believe ourselves to be, and why we typically get only what we believe we deserve. The problem is that our beliefs about ourselves are often based on what *others* think about us, and consequently, we let others define our lives.

It happens all the time. Most of us frequently scan the environment, looking for indications that we are smart, funny, kind, or beautiful. If the feedback says we are, then we believe it. And if the feedback says we aren't, then that belief becomes our own.

That's a mistake. Some people will like you, and some won't. Some people will find you attractive, but not everyone. And when you let other people define your beliefs, who knows what you will end up believing?

Don't let others determine your life. Take full ownership of who you are and what you are capable of. Make your beliefs your own.

> *Argue for your limitations, and sure enough, they're yours.*
>
> **—Richard Bach**

It is a source of great trouble in the world: The ignorant are so cocksure, while the competent are full of doubt. The same knowledge that can enable success can also produce an inner dialogue full of self-criticism, constantly reminding us of all the reasons why we can't be successful.

How could I possibly be a writer? you may ask yourself.

Why do I deserve to be a successful inventor or entrepreneur?

Who am I to have these dreams?

Well, who are you *not* to?

Why we find it so difficult to turn ourselves into our own biggest supporter isn't always clear. But negative self-talk doesn't *have* to push us around.

Start examining the way you think about yourself and your life. And begin removing any self-imposed perceptions that may be limiting your progress.

If you keep telling yourself you can't do something, that perception is sure to become reality.

> *In the kingdom of the blind, the one-eyed man is king.*
>
> **—Desiderius Erasmus**

Many things in life are beyond your control: you cannot determine your genetics, your family, your country of birth, or the economy. But you can control your perceptions, which happen to be far more important when it comes to achieving success.

Indeed, a difference in perception is often the reason why two people can face the same circumstances yet achieve entirely different outcomes. The underlying reason why is because of our RAS—our reticular activating system.

The RAS is part of the brain. It connects the brain stem to the cerebral cortex. And it seeks to create a reality that is aligned with our thoughts: it strives to bring into our lives whatever we spend the most energy focusing on—good or bad. Whether it's a promotion, a holiday, a house, or our shortcomings, failures, and fears, our RAS will do its best to guide us toward that reality.

That's why we must ask ourselves: do I spend more time and energy thinking about the great possibilities of the future, or bemoaning the problems of the present? Whichever it is, that will be the focus of your RAS—and, hence, your future reality.

Living among the blind, you need only one eye to rise above the rest. But when everyone has two eyes, any difference comes from *how* you perceive the world.

Everyone admits that "the truth hurts" but no one applies this adage to himself—and as soon as it begins to hurt us, we quickly repudiate it and call it a lie. It is this tendency toward self-deception (more than any active sin) that makes human progress slow and almost imperceptible.

—**Sydney J. Harris**

How you approach life's challenges is a major determining factor in how you perform. If you expect to win, you are more likely to win. If you believe you are capable of performing, you are more likely to perform capably. But let's be clear: successful people believe they can, but they are far from delusional.

Perceiving the world to your advantage does not mean denying reality or hiding the truth from yourself. It means seeking out and confronting reality, all the while believing success is possible, and knowing that there is a positive side to every situation.

If things aren't so great right now, don't pretend they are. The consequences of self-deception are as chilling as the benefits of intelligent perception are thrilling. The worst part is, self-deception is a *self-inflicted* wound.

Be candid with yourself: Are you in good physical shape? Are your relationships as fulfilling as they could be? Is your job the one you really want?

Face the facts and confront your problems, while still believing that you *can* achieve your goals. That's how you move forward.

Why Not You?

Life can be much broader once you discover one simple fact: Everything around you that you call life was made up by people who were no smarter than you. And you can change it, you can influence it . . . Once you learn that, you'll never be the same again.

—**Steve Jobs**

When you set goals for yourself—especially if they are ambitious and challenging—some people will tell you that you're taking too big a bite. It's impossible; the task is too big; you're not qualified; you don't have the skills.

Sometimes, people do this out of true concern and love for you. But often, people do so because they have given up on their own dreams and subconsciously want you to do the same.

Be smart about letting others' opinions influence your perceptions. Consider the facts, but realize that your friends and family may not be able to see what you can see. Thomas Edison didn't give up in his quest for an incandescent lightbulb. Nor did the Wright Brothers ever give up on their dream of powered flight. And they had some doubters, to say the least.

Those who believe that they can change the world are the only ones who do.

It is not a lucky word, this name "impossible": no good comes of those that have it so often in their mouths.

—**Thomas Carlyle**

How do we arrive at the decision that something is impossible, that a goal is too far out of reach, that success is something we can't attain?

If we take an honest look, we generally find scant evidence for our paltry assessment of what we can or cannot achieve. Dig a little more, and we're apt to find that our perceptions of what's possible have been shaped largely by what *others* think.

Critical to perceiving the world to your advantage is the awareness that history is filled with stories of those who accomplished what others thought "impossible." Impossible bridges have been built. Impossible mountains have been climbed. Impossible oceans have been crossed. And impossible space has been voyaged.

We cannot comprehend what we cannot imagine. Don't let other people's perceptions of what is possible dictate your life.

The question is not, "How intelligent are you?" The question is, "How are you intelligent?"

—Ken Robinson

People often give up on their dreams because they perceive themselves as lacking in intellectual capacity—they suppose that they are not smart enough. This is partly due to the ubiquity of standardized testing, which heavily favors analytical and logical thinking and reasoning over, say, creative thinking.

Don't let that cloud your perceptions. Each of us has a natural aptitude in certain areas of life, and each of us is intelligent, just in different ways.

Maybe you excel at structured problem solving, while public speaking is your worst nightmare. Or you can multiply six-digit numbers in your head but struggle to read Shakespeare. Or perhaps you are like Bocelli, a world-class talent who needs help crossing a busy street.

You have the potential for greatness. But first, ponder where your strengths lie and your ambition seeks to lead you.

Our deepest fear is not that we are inadequate. Our deepest fear is that we are powerful beyond measure. It is our light, not our darkness, that most frightens us. We ask ourselves, "Who am I to be brilliant, gorgeous, talented, and fabulous?" Actually, who are you not to be? You are a child of God. Your playing small does not serve the world. There is nothing enlightened about shrinking so that other people will not feel insecure around you.

—Marianne Williamson

Some people seem to be born believing that they can do almost anything. But for most of us, it's different. It takes us time to recognize, accept, and believe that we have the potential to be great.

If you want to speed up the process, take a closer look at the perceptions you hold of yourself, others, and the world. Do you see yourself as competent and worthy of success, or as someone destined to fail? Do you perceive people as being on your side, or out to get you? Is the world trying to crush your dreams, or help you reach them?

Once you've answered those questions, stress-test any perceptions that may be hindering your success. Is what you perceive founded on facts, or on something that you have conjured up?

Take the time to explore yourself. You don't want to arrive at the end of your life and realize you did but a fraction of what you could have done—and, worst of all, because of self-imposed limitations.

Who are you *not* to be brilliant?

The more leaders I have the privilege of meeting, the more I realize that they are no different from you or me. They are simply men and women determined to make the greatest impact they can in the time they have.

—Jay Samit

Even the most astonishing success stories reveal the same underlying pattern: an accumulation of thousands of small positive decisions and actions that, over time, added up to something magnificent.

This reflects the fact that the great achievers of the world are fundamentally no different from you or me. The difference between the few and the many is that the many often lack (1) a belief that success is possible for them, and (2) the determination and self-discipline to endure through the "little" tasks—the tasks that add up over time and lead to amazing achievement.

If you believe in yourself and are determined to achieve your goals, success is not only possible, it's all but guaranteed.

A man may appear to the world as a marvel: yet his wife and his manservant see nothing remarkable about him. Few men have been wonders to their families.

—Michel de Montaigne

Whether it be Isaac Newton or Albert Einstein, William Shakespeare or Friedrich Nietzsche, Joan of Arc, Catherine the Great, Helen Keller, or Mother Teresa, the greats are mere mortals like the rest of us.

The problem is that we build them up in our minds to be more than they are. We are too far removed from their lives to see that they, too, grow old; they, too, have fears and doubts, foibles, and insecurities; and they, too, are *human*. And when we distinguish between them and ourselves, we often place success out of our own reach.

Who gave you the idea that you can't become one of the greats?

The Beauty of Life

Everything has its wonders, even darkness and silence, and I learn, whatever state I may be in, therein to be content.

—Helen Keller

Technology has resulted in great leaps in productivity. It has also improved health, education, and access to finance in even the remotest areas of the Earth. On top of that, we now live in a world that is truly nonstop. It never even slows down. We are always connected, and our phones, computers, and smart watches make sure we don't miss a beat. The problem is, we can get so caught up with everything that's going on, we forget to appreciate the beauty of life itself.

Perceiving the world to your advantage is not just about looking for the silver lining and believing that success is possible for you. It's also about looking for the sublime in the ordinary.

No matter how fast paced your life may be, learn to see the beauty, experience the wonder, and feel the joy that exists in every moment. It's there. But you have to look for it.

Only by seeing the world anew, as fresh and strange as it once was to the ancients who saw it first, can we both re-create it and preserve it for the future.

—Peter Thiel

We often see the world through a lens of preconceived ideas (biases) that are the result of our upbringing. This baggage disconnects us from the beauty and joy that is alive in the world. It is the difference between a child who is charmed by a simple flower, and an adult who wanders the hallways of the Musée du Louvre and feels nothing.

Bring awareness into your thoughts. Are you truly seeing the world, or are your eyes open but glazed over? Do you notice the snow slowly drifting down? The sun, rising up from behind a mountain? Or a shaft of moonlight shining into the room?

To see the world as if for the first time is a beautiful experience.

> *It takes a great deal of courage to see the world in all its tainted glory, and still to love it.*
>
> **—Oscar Wilde**

The world has a lot of pain and suffering. Hatred, angst, prejudice, and fear are to be found almost everywhere. But there is also a lot of joy. And a lot of love, kindness, tolerance, and faith.

Intelligent perception is not about shielding yourself from the "bad." It's about looking beyond the bad and finding the positive, wherever you are and whatever the circumstances. It's also about appreciating that our character doesn't develop in the easy times: transformational growth is found in the fiery flames, deep recesses, and dark waters of life.

Life has some warts, but still it is beautiful.

And so . . .

Your perceptions influence your thoughts. Your thoughts define your beliefs. Your beliefs determine your actions. Your actions shape your habits. Your habits form your character. And your character dictates your life. That's how perception leads to reality. And that's why perceiving the world to your advantage is so important.

Choose to perceive life's challenges and failures *not* as insurmountable obstacles and unalterable end results, but as opportunities for growth and learning. And choose to fill your mind *not* with dream-deflating, ambition-curbing negativity, but with inspiring and motivating thoughts and perceptions.

This is not delusion. It is an intentional, growth-oriented perception of yourself, others, and the world. It is the recognition that through your mind, through the way you perceive the world, you are the architect of your life.

Not only are you the architect. You are also the experiencer. And your perceptions can either conceal or bring into focus the beauty of life hidden in the ordinary.

Life *is* beautiful, magnificent, wondrous, but we become numb to it. The image we see of the world enters through the cornea, travels to the retina, goes up the optic nerve, and reaches our brain, where we catalog it and file it under "seen that already." In doing so, we blind ourselves to the majesty of life that is going on right in front of us.

To create and live the best life you can, learn to perceive the world to your advantage.

Always Strive for Growth

Become All that You Can

Forever Room to Grow

Growth of the Heart, Soul, and Mind

The Arenas of Growth

SUCCESS IS ABOUT what you become, not what you get. This is why the essence of success is growth: growth of the heart, the mind, the soul.

"Growth" doesn't mean radically changing yourself (although, in some circumstances, that may be the best path forward). But it does mean refining your philosophy on growth.

Start striving to become all that you can be. Commit yourself now to the unending pursuit of knowledge and wisdom, forever identifying the information you need, acquiring it, drawing your own conclusions from it, and then applying it to improve your life and the lives of others. There is forever room to grow.

And start welcoming discomfort, for you can't grow without it. Only by leaving your comfort zone—that safe place where you feel in control—can you test your strength, expand your capabilities, and grow.

The relentless pursuit of growth isn't easy, but it is possible. It takes courage, self-discipline, and a continuing refinement of your philosophy. But nothing else compares to the rewards from a life of growth. Nothing else is quite like the contentment experienced by those who know that they did all they could, and gave all they had.

Become All that You Can

> *The aim of life is self-development. To realize one's nature perfectly—that is what each of us is here for. People are afraid of themselves, nowadays. They have forgotten the highest of all duties, the duty that one owes to oneself.*
>
> **—Oscar Wilde**

Self-development is the best gift you can give yourself. It's also the best gift you can give others. For the more wisdom you gain, the more skills you acquire, and the more you grow, the better the friend, spouse, sibling, or colleague you can become.

It's the great challenge of life: to continually strive to become more today than we were yesterday, and to develop into the highest version of ourselves that we are capable of being. But it's a challenge we must meet, because it is through self-development that we create a better life for ourselves and those around us. And it is through self-development that we accomplish our dreams.

Miss a meal, but don't neglect your self-development.

> *Go for the challenge and the responsibility of being the absolute best you can . . . Make all the friends you can, read as many books as you can, develop as many skills as you can, see and do as much as possible, make as much of a fortune as possible, give as much of it away as possible. Strive for the maximum; there's no life like it!*
>
> **—Jim Rohn**

To develop to our full potential—mentally, emotionally, and spiritually—is what success is all about. It's a never-ending pursuit.

When we meet someone who is *wildly* successful, their relentless pursuit for growth is clear. We see the passion in their eyes, and we feel the uncontrollable desire that lives within them. It doesn't matter how old they are or what they have; they are unyielding in their search for growth.

Our lives are forever changing. But are we evolving? Strive to evolve from who you are today into someone even greater tomorrow.

The most important investment you can make is in yourself. Very few people get anything like their potential horsepower translated into the actual horsepower of their output in life. Potential exceeds realization for many people . . . The best asset is your own self.

—Warren Buffett

It is easy to see what people are committed to and what they value. All you need do is look at where they invest their time and money. You know what else is easy? Judging others—and overlooking ourselves.

How many books have you read this year? How much time have you spent working on your health? When did you last conduct a detailed review of your finances? (I told you, judging others is easy!)

Learning, improving your health, and being fiscally disciplined cost money, effort, and time, yes. But they are less expensive, less painful, and less time consuming than ignorance and neglect.

Take the time, spend the money, and invest in *you*. Invest in your self-education. Invest in your personal development. Invest in your future.

If the greatest investor who ever lived should advise you to invest in yourself, would you listen?

I tried to persuade each one of you to concern himself less with what he has than with what he is, so as to render himself as excellent and rational as possible.

—Socrates

It is who you are, not what you have, that is valuable. That's why personal development—developing your skills, expanding your capabilities, and sculpting your character to become your highest possible self—is so important.

In life, you attract what you are. When you are a person of integrity, you attract others of integrity. When you are someone with influence, you attract others who are influential. On the other hand, if you are floundering through life, you will find plenty of others to flounder with you.

Make sure you work on improving yourself. Not only will you become more, but the network that surrounds you will strengthen, too.

If you work hard on your job, you can become great at something. If you work hard on *yourself*, you can become something great.

There is no passion to be found playing small—in settling for a life that is less than the one you are capable of living.

—Nelson Mandela

To live true to ourselves and develop to our full potential is a dream for many but a reality for few. Even though we realize intellectually that we should strive for the best life we can create, we continue plodding on with a life that is anything but.

Part of the reason why is that most of us won't risk what we have today for the opportunity to have something greater tomorrow. And the longer we wait, the harder it becomes to take our roots out of the ground and plant them somewhere new. The question is, what are you willing to risk for the chance to live an extraordinary life?

It takes courage to strive always for growth. But if you wish to live the life you dream of, courage is what you must find.

> *To live is the rarest thing in the world. Most people exist, that is all.*
>
> **—Oscar Wilde**

Few of us will get close to reaching our full potential in life. We tend to blame this on anything besides ourselves, but the truth is that *we* hold ourselves back—by not striving for growth every day.

What a tragedy! For we live in a marvelous world that most of us have seen only a small fraction of. And let's not forget the wonderful journey available for each of us to embark on: the exploration of our own mind.

Look around you. Is it life you see, or simply existence? The point is not to judge, but to learn. You have only this one fragile life, and it's up to you to make the most of it.

To *live*, or exist. It's your choice.

> **Good is the enemy of great.**
>
> **—Unknown**

Many people achieve moderate success in life, but that's about it. There are two mutually reinforcing reasons for this. The first is that the more we have, the more we desire preservation over growth. That is, the closer we get to our full potential, the more likely we are to cease growing.

The second reason is that we are loss averse: we feel the pain of loss more than we feel the joy of gain. This leads us to fear losing what we have more than we desire winning what we might get.

For these two reasons, most people settle for the "good" life they have today instead of striving for a potentially greater life tomorrow. If you are truly content with what you have right now, this is less important. But if you desire more from life, then you must do your best to overcome both these hindrances.

Regular reflection (more on this soon) can counter the first. Make sure to monitor the *rate* of progress toward your goals. If you find yourself slowing, investigate why.

Objective risk appraisal can quell the second. Translating your thoughts from mind to paper helps to impartially assess a situation. And try to focus equitably on the downside *and* the upside.

Beware the "good" life. It is the enemy of the great life.

Forever Room to Grow

There is only one way to be in serious trouble today, and that is not to be trying, not to be failing, not to be stretching yourself.

—Tom Peters

When you arise in the morning, how do you approach the day? Are you trying to make it *through* the day? Or are you trying to get *from* the day? Every day holds opportunity to grow, develop, and stretch ourselves. And each day is a gift that we either use or lose.

The first keyword in that sentence was "gift." The rising of the sun each morning won't change anytime soon, but whether you are there to witness it is a different story.

The other keyword was "use." Why not get *from* the day? Why not try to learn something and improve, even if it's just by 1 percent? Get a little wiser, get a little healthier, get a little more skilled. Do this daily, and with patience and persistence, you can create whatever life you desire.

The greatest distances are covered by those with a steady march.

Near this spot

    are deposited the Remains of one

who possessed Beauty without Vanity,

    Strength without Insolence,

Courage without Ferocity,

    and all the virtues of Man without his Vices.

This praise, which would be unmeaning Flattery

    if inscribed over human Ashes,

is but a just tribute to the Memory of

    Boatswain, a dog . . .

—George Gordon Byron

We humans are the most advanced species on Earth. But even a cursory inspection of some of the supposedly lesser species suggests that we still have much to learn and much growth ahead of us.

Consider a dog, living completely and freely in each moment. Unattached, unresisting, one with the flow of the universe. Might there be a lesson here for us?

What about the green anaconda of tropical South America? Waiting patiently, hour after hour, day after day, until the opportune moment to strike appears. If only we could have such patience and persistence.

There is forever room to grow. Examples that guide the way can be found almost everywhere.

As for me, all I know is that I know nothing.

—**Socrates**

Socrates was among the wisest of his time. Yet, he claims to know nothing? Why? Because the more we know, the more we realize how little we know.

That's why there is no limit to how much you can learn. There's no limit to how deeply you can feel. And there's no limit to the contribution you can make to the world. But without experience, it can be difficult to see all that you are capable of becoming—to see the possibilities of the future.

That's part of the journey of life. And as you accomplish more, you'll begin to see how much more you are capable of accomplishing. In the meantime, know that there is always more knowledge to gain, skills to acquire, and room to grow.

Growth of the Heart, Soul, and Mind

Let sad things make you sad; let happy things make you happy . . . Let the emotion strike you . . . Our emotions need to be as educated as our intellect. It's important to know how to feel. It's important to know how to respond. It's important to let life in.

—Jim Rohn

What is the point of bungee jumping if you get no thrill? There's no point. Why wake up early to watch the sunrise, or stay up late to gaze at the mystical night sky, if your heart and soul aren't moved? There's no reason. And why be alive at all, if you can't feel a thing?

Growth of the heart is just as important as growth of the mind. Life is no more than the breadth and depth of emotions that we experience on our journey. Life is measured by the intensity of the highs that we feel after great achievement, and also by the potency of the soul-wrenching lows that envelop us when we fail.

Wherever you find yourself, open the door to your heart and let life in. After a big achievement, celebrate and revel in the flow of positive emotions. And if you miss out on your dream job, let the disappointment stay with you for a little while. Let it teach you how it feels to fail. It is from the joy of winning and the pain of losing, that we grow.

Start educating your emotions. To feel deeply and with appreciation takes practice.

I believe that, if we are honest with ourselves, the most fascinating problem in the world is "Who am I?"

—Alan Watts

Who, or what, are you? And what are you doing here? Those are *big* questions. They are also important questions—ones that inspire people to change everything in their life.

But what tends to happen is that the answers to those questions are "given" to us at a young age, and we never take the time to investigate them ourselves.

From the minute we enter this world, the environment we are in is shaping us. In a few years, we learn to walk, speak, and gesture like those around us. We are almost as quick to adopt the spiritual beliefs of our parents, just as our parents took on their parents' beliefs. And so we find, unsurprisingly, that our spiritual beliefs are the same as those that predominate in the culture we were brought up in. That's why someone born in the West is likely to be a Christian; in the Middle-East, a Muslim; and in mainland Southeast Asia, a Buddhist (generally speaking).

There's a certain logic to that: children need structure to guide them in their early years, and adults need answers to the persnickety questions that children ask. But there comes a time to start exploring spirituality for *yourself.*

That means you stop simply accepting what others tell you is gospel, and you stop following the crowd simply because there is a crowd. Instead, you venture into the depths of your soul and seek out the answers to those big life-questions, of your own accord.

Who are you?

What can we gain by sailing to the moon if we are not able to cross the abyss that separates us from ourselves? This is the most important of all voyages of discovery, and without it, all the rest are not only useless, but disastrous.

—Thomas Merton

The successful life is a journey of discovery. It is a navigation of both the external world and your inner world. And although you may accomplish your goals without deepening the understanding of yourself, it is far less likely and also far less fulfilling. More importantly, to arrive at life's end having neglected the opportunity to explore the inner workings of your own mind and heart and soul, is to have lived but half a life.

There is a huge, wonderful world out there. And there is also one right inside you. Why not take a look?

> *The illustrious ancients, when they wished to make clear and to propagate the highest virtues in the world, put their states in proper order. Before putting their states in proper order, they regulated their families. Before regulating their families, they cultivated their own selves. Before cultivating their own selves, they perfected their souls. Before perfecting their souls, they tried to be sincere in their thoughts. Before trying to be sincere in their thoughts, they extended to the utmost their knowledge.*
>
> **—Confucius**

Trace time back far enough, and we reach the origin of the universe: the single point from which everything arose. Trace success back far enough, and we reach another origin: the birth of knowledge in the mind, which gave rise to an idea.

Knowledge not only engenders success; it also determines the magnitude of it. That's why it is so important to study both your life and the greater world.

Study your life. Seek to understand your ambitions and desires, strengths and weaknesses, and motivations and temptations. In doing so, you create clarity in what you want and how you operate.

Study the world. Learn the history of humankind, earth, the universe. Read about the tragedies of life. Analyze the failures. Examine the successes. Do this, and you will begin to see the many different paths available for you to achieve your goals.

From study comes knowledge. From knowledge come ideas. And from ideas comes success.

> *Consider [education] not as the painful accumulation of facts and dates, but as an ennobling intimacy with great men. Consider it not as the preparation of the individual to make a living, but as the development of every potential capacity in him for the comprehension, control and appreciation of his world.*
>
> **—Will Durant**

Most people will agree that education is important. But what some seem to have forgotten is that education is far more than a diploma or a university transcript. Such items represent only one part of what it means to be educated.

There are three parts to education. The first part is an understanding of all the knowledge we have acquired. That's what a diploma or transcript can signify.

The second part is knowing how we can *apply* that knowledge to improve our life and the lives of others. (Sadly, they don't hand out diplomas for that.)

The last part is being aware of the knowledge we currently lack—the knowledge we still need to acquire—to achieve our goals. This part is equally as important as the others.

Three good questions to ask: To create the life I desire, what information do I need? What am I currently lacking? And how can I get it?

> *It is clear to you, I am sure, Lucilius, that no man can live a happy life, or even a supportable life, without the study of wisdom.*

> **—Seneca**

Before we can be wise, we must study wisdom. Before we can be influential, we must study influence. And before we can be successful, we must study success. Indeed, study comes before all else.

But make sure to strike a balance in the information you gather. We can't just be inspired; we must also be challenged. We can't just be motivated; we must also be educated.

And the process doesn't stop at studying. Once you have the information, put it into practice and, ideally, teach others. (Teaching reinforces learning like little else can.)

Whatever you want in life, the information on how to get it is out there, and it's easier to access today than ever before.

> *In today's knowledge-based economy, what you earn depends on what you learn.*

> **—Bill Clinton**

With the advent of the Internet, more people have access to more information than ever before in history. And as you would expect, our collective intelligence has grown. But it's a two-edged sword: as the average intelligence quotient rises, so does the average level of competitiveness.

That's why continued education is so important. But as we enter into an ever more fluid future, we must revise the way we educate ourselves, so our methods are better aligned with today's world.

Don't limit your education to the skills needed for a single job. Don't acquire only the knowledge that helps you excel where you are today. Instead, seek the knowledge that will take you toward the future you desire.

And don't restrict yourself to formal education. Learning doesn't have to be formalized. Every situation presents a chance to learn about ourselves, others, or the world. Opportunity for less formal, but no less valuable, learning is all around us.

There are more players on the field, and they are smarter than ever before. If you want keep up with the curve, keep up with your education.

Any fool can know. The point is to understand.

—Unknown

Knowledge and understanding are different things. Knowledge is no more than information you have acquired. It may help you win a round of Trivial Pursuit or sound smart among your friends, but by itself it is not tremendously useful.

On the other hand, understanding is knowledge that you have *transformed* so you can use it to improve your life and the lives of others. The genesis of understanding begins with the question: What worthwhile things can I do with this knowledge?

For growth of the mind, seek to expand your knowledge, but don't neglect to develop your understanding. We must *apply* what we learn.

You cannot teach a man anything; you can only help him to find it within himself.

—Galileo Galilei

Galileo suggests that nothing worth knowing can be taught; it must be discovered through personal experience. In other words, we cannot grow through theory alone; we can grow only through practice.

To an extent, this is true, for we never truly know an experience until we have lived through it. We cannot know love by reading about it, any more than we can become leaders by studying leadership principles. But learning from the experiences of others is still important. It's like a preparatory course that enables us to extract more value, faster and with less pain, when we eventually experience the situation.

Great men and women have come and gone long before us. Why not learn from them? Why not let them teach you?

> *And when at some future date the high court of history sits in judgment on each of us . . . we will be measured by the answers to four questions:*
>
> > *First, were we truly men of courage . . .*
> >
> > *Second, were we truly men of judgment . . .*
> >
> > *Third, were we truly men of integrity . . .*
> >
> > *Finally, were we truly men of dedication . . .*
>
> *Courage—judgment—integrity—dedication—these are the historic qualities.*
>
> **—John F. Kennedy**

Today, we are of greater average intelligence than at any other time in history, and we should make the most of the deep reservoir of knowledge that we now have at our fingertips. But we should also be wondering, what of our character? Have we become better men and women? It's difficult to say.

Character represents the union of heart, mind, and soul. It is one of the most important—and most overlooked—aspects of growth. Part of the reason why is that there is no universal agreement on what "character" specifically means.

Each society uses some combination of attractive qualities—honesty, trust, faith, integrity, wisdom, and so on—to describe what it means to be a man or woman of character. But the criteria can change as we move between different societies. In the Western world, it is unlikely that a polygamist would be described as someone of character. But within the Maasai tribe of Tanzania, such a man could be revered.

The criteria for being a person of character can also change within the same society over time. Consider the United States during the eighteenth and nineteenth centuries versus today. Before the Civil War, many men and women who were considered upstanding citizens participated freely and willingly in the abomination that is slavery. And would you or I have acted any differently had we been in their position?

Let's simplify: Strive to live true to yourself in thought, word, and action. Strive to embody the qualities that you respect in others. And strive to become someone you are proud to be.

Success achieved at your own or others' expense is inevitably short-lived and unfulfilling. At some point, we all must look in the mirror.

The Arenas of Growth

He who wrestles with us, strengthens our nerves and sharpens our skills. Our antagonist is our helper.

—Edmund Burke

Why the turmoil? Why the turbulence? Why the seemingly endless struggle just to keep our head above water? We may never have an answer, but one thing is clear: it is through challenge and adversity that we grow, and discomfort is the signal that says we've entered the arena.

Indeed, after enough time has passed, when you reflect on those difficult periods in your life—a rejected college application, a failed business venture, a missed promotion—you can see just how much you grew from them.

They walk toward us as an illusory foe. They sit down with us, placing their bag of unpleasantness right on the table. They leave us cursing their name. And later we recall them fondly, now aware that this foe was a friend that helped us to grow into someone greater than we were. Such is the story of challenge, adversity, and discomfort.

It is when things are difficult, when temptation is staring you right in the face, that you prove your strength.

—Darren Hardy

Growth—mental, emotional, and spiritual—comes when we are knocked down. For it is in times of trial that we test ourselves, stretch our capabilities, and find out what we are made of.

Such situations aren't always pleasant while we are in them. (Few of us like crawling out of a warm bed for a five a.m. training session, or doing our first speech before a large audience.) But these are often the experiences we look back on with gratitude for how they transformed us into who we are today.

When you're in the thick of it, try to see the situation as an opportunity. Try to remember that you are in the arena of growth—*right now*. And remind yourself that no matter how bad things get, you'll get through it and you'll be stronger for it.

> *In a growth environment, you are often out of your comfort zone.*
>
> **—John C. Maxwell**

There is no growth without discomfort, for we grow only when we push ourselves, extend our capabilities, and leave our comfort zone. And there is also no discomfort without risk.

The problem is that our biology pushes us to seek *preservation* of self over *growth* of self. Meaning we are biologically wired to avoid taking risks. This is because humans have spent most of their time in an earlier world lacking law and civilized society—a place where risk taking tended to have swift and deadly consequences. For that reason, we learned to avoid risk wherever we could.

But today the world is different, and concerns of imminent death are no longer valid for those of us fortunate enough to live in a safe place. Yet we limit ourselves and the growth we can achieve, by listening too attentively to these outdated biological instincts.

If you are looking for accelerated growth, update your mind-set on risk: take yourself out of your comfort zone as often as you can.

Men are carried away by their passions, their actions not being preceded by reflection: these are the men who walk in darkness. On the other hand, the philosopher, even in his passions, acts only after reflection; he walks in the dark, but by a torch.

—**Denis Diderot**

Imagine life as a big, dark room that you are standing in the middle of. Then think of success as where you want to go in that room, and what you want to find. And let's say you've got some light with you, to help guide your way.

That's a relief, right? Because a little light in a dark room makes a big difference: the difference between stumbling around like a fool and eventually getting to where you want to go, finding what you want to find.

Now, if life represents the room, and success represents where you want to go and what you want to find, then what does the light represent? The light represents *reflection*—a powerful tool that enables you to leverage your past experiences so that they can guide you in the present, toward the future you desire.

Reflection starts with thinking about your past. What did you do last week, last month, last year? What did you do well? What did you do poorly? What did you learn?

Once you have gathered the teachings from your past, look to your future: Where do you want to go? And what do you need to get there?

Then, with the teachings from your past and the dreams for your future in hand, bring your thoughts back to the present: What is the best course of action to take *right now*?

Make sure you reflect on every year. But try also to reflect on every month, every week, and every day. The more you reflect, the more you learn, and the more deeply you understand yourself.

It helps—indeed, it is crucial—to make use of a journal. You need a place to note down all the good ideas that come to you, capture all that you have learned while you are in the moment, and record your journey so that it can serve you—and perhaps others—in the future. The importance of this cannot be overstated.

If you want some light to help guide your way in life, start harnessing the power of reflection.

And so . . .

Growth is hard. Always striving for growth is even harder. But if you wish to develop to your full potential, to live life to the hilt, and to make most of all you've been given, then it is a challenge you must meet.

Time will only accelerate. So no matter where you are on your journey, make a conscious effort to grow every day. Expose yourself to a variety of philosophies, cultures, people, and values. Give your heart, soul, and mind the nourishment they need for growth.

And courageously venture into the arenas of growth. Welcome challenge. Greet adversity for the friend in disguise that it really is. Embrace discomfort. And be self-disciplined with the process that ties together the past, present, and future: the process of reflection.

You can achieve far more than you ever believed possible. But only if you continue to learn and discover more about yourself, others, and the world. Only if you strive *always* for growth.

Set Your Goals, Then Plan and Execute

Success Starts with Setting Goals

Find Out What Matters to You

Don't Underestimate Yourself

Planning Is Paramount

No Action, No Success

Executing Isn't Easy

HERE'S A SIMPLIFIED formula for success: set wise goals, make sound plans, and take action.

The first step, setting goals, begins with introspection. It's tremendously important to take the time to look within yourself and ask: What do I truly desire? Or, put differently, if I could do anything with my life, what would that be? It's one of the most vital questions you can ever ask. Indeed, it will lay the foundation for all your goals.

After introspection comes imagination. Dare to dream the greatest life you can imagine. Think *bigger*, in both the what and the when. Set goals for this month, this year, and next year, yes, but also think about where you want to be ten, twenty, thirty years from today.

The second step is planning. Planning is critical because it focuses your mind and creates clarity on how you will achieve your goals. Planning also breaks your goals down into manageable pieces, helping you see that they are possible to achieve. And the best part is, plans don't need to be complex.

Finally, and perhaps most importantly, we must execute. Dreams, goals, and plans without action are but a pipe dream. Results are what count in life, and we achieve them by executing.

But it isn't going to be easy. Life is going to throw some curveballs at you when you least expect them. The key to executing is persistence: to continue working toward your goals, little by little, no matter what happens.

This is where desire becomes paramount. For only if you truly desire something will you have the drive to push past the inevitable challenges of the journey and bring your dreams into reality.

Your life will be no better than the goals you set, the plans you make, and the actions you take. And each of us must suffer pain of one kind or the other: the pain of self-discipline or the pain of regret. You get to choose which it will be.

Success Starts with Setting Goals

Setting goals is the first step in turning the invisible into the visible.

—Tony Robbins

Many people wander aimlessly through life, never setting goals and never experiencing the joy of seeing their dreams come to life. But if you don't know where you want to go or what you want to achieve in the next year, two years, or five years, how do you expect to get there?

As simple as it sounds, a fundamental part of success is setting a goal and then writing it down. It's not enough to have a goal. *You must write it down.* Why? Because it's the best way to keep yourself focused and accountable.

There are many different frameworks you can use for this. But whichever one you choose, make sure you have both short- and long-term goals. Short-term goals help build your confidence, because you see the process working for you. And long-term goals keep you aimed in the right direction.

It also helps to organize your goals into appropriate categories. Yours may include personal development (skills you want to learn), economics (wealth), relationships (with family, friends, a romantic partner), spirituality, health and fitness, career, entrepreneurial endeavors, community, and happiness. (Yes, happiness deserves its own bucket.) The key is to find a system that works for you, and to review your goals daily.

The greatest achievement was at first and for a time a dream. The oak sleeps in the acorn; the bird waits in the egg; and in the highest vision of the soul a waking angel stirs. Dreams are the seedlings of realities.

—James Allen

The factors that influence our lives are too many and varied to count: the circumstances of our birth, the country we grew up in, the schools we attended, our friends and family, and every experience we have ever had. But only one factor accounts for the fundamental difference between those who scrape by and those who live an uncommon life.

That crucial difference is the ability to *dream*: the ability to create a vision so clear and vivid that it inspires us to do *whatever* it takes, to turn that dream into reality.

Let's not get confused. Dreams aren't fleeting thoughts that come and go like fair-weather friends. Dreams are enduring, persistent, withstanding any force. It's as if they were etched into the neural pathways of our brains.

That's why dreams have underpinned every major development in human history. They have led us from caves to cities, from superstition to science, across oceans and to the moon. And they will continue to lead humankind to ever greater heights.

Your future achievements—your future life—will begin in your mind as a dream.

Find Out What Matters to You

My uniqueness, I realized, came in the specifics of all the dreams—from incredibly meaningful to decidedly quirky—that defined my forty-six years of life. Sitting there, I knew that despite the cancer, I truly believed I was a lucky man because I had lived out these dreams.

—**Randy Pausch**

It's a good strategy in life to identify the end result you desire, and then work backward from there to determine what you must do to achieve it.

What's the perfect endgame for your life? If your last day on this planet were finally to arrive, what would make you say to yourself, "I succeeded"? Perhaps a certain net worth, or a term at the helm of a Fortune 500 company, would do it. Or having done something tangible to reduce poverty, improve literacy, or tackle some health issue somewhere in the world. Or maybe you desire no less than to raise a loving, caring, and happy family.

Once you have the answer, the next step is to determine what this means for how you must live your life. What do you need to do, what goals do you need to set, to achieve your desired outcome? Then—and here is the hard part—how do you transition from the life you are living now to the life that gets you to your desired end state?

Make what matters your focus.

*What would you like to do if money were no object? . . .
Better to have a short life that is full of what you like doing than a long life spent in a miserable way.*

—**Alan Watts**

To live a life of fulfillment and contentment, we must do what we love. There is no other way. The problem is that we often stop ourselves from making the life changes that will allow us to follow our dreams. Why do we stop ourselves? Usually, because of money.

Money can spur us on or paralyze us. Its charm can empower us to do and experience great things. But it can also get in our way, casting fear into our mind—should we lose that weekly salary check—thus preventing us from following our heart and chasing our dreams.

When setting your goals, ask yourself: What would I do if I had all the money I ever needed? Some people might tell you this is an unrealistic approach to life. But devoting yourself to your passion could be your best financial move, notwithstanding a wise decision for your happiness.

That's because the income we receive reflects the value we add to the market. And one of the best ways to add enormous value is by dedicating ourselves to a craft we love, honing that craft, and then offering that craft to others. Simply put: you will work far harder chasing your dreams than you would doing something that feels like "just a job."

Let money entice you, but don't let it restrain you from your dreams.

> *The most powerful weapon on earth is the human soul on fire.*
>
> **—Ferdinand Foch**

We can't be successful unless we do what we love. And as those souls in the final stages of life will tell you, it's far better to fail while chasing your passion than to succeed at something you don't enjoy.

So if you've found your passion in life, wonderful! But if you haven't, don't let that keep you from setting goals.

There are two reasons why: First, you'll find your passion when the time is right, as long as you listen to your intuition and pay close attention to your life. And second, giving it your all and doing your best—no matter what you are doing—builds a reputation that will serve you greatly when you do find your passion.

Until that time comes, be passionate about learning new skills, seizing opportunities, and growing in health, wealth, and wisdom. Be passionate about creating and living an extraordinary life.

Don't Underestimate Yourself

The greatest danger for most of us is not that our aim is too high and we miss it, but that it is too low and we reach it.

—Michelangelo

The world you see reflects the experiences you have had in your life. And because we all are limited in our experiences, what we perceive to be possible—both for us and for those around us—is often but a glimpse of reality.

Try to think *bigger*. What could you accomplish if you really applied yourself over the next ten years? Give yourself the chance to rise to the challenge, and you will find within you the ability to do remarkable things. For wherever we set the bar and whatever the expectations, we humans can extend ourselves to meet the demands of the situation—sometimes in an astonishing manner.

The success you can achieve—mentally, emotionally, and spiritually—is far greater than what you can see right now. So dream your grandest dream and then multiply by ten. *Now* you have a goal.

Life is too brief to think small.

My interest in life comes from setting myself huge, apparently unachievable challenges, and trying to rise above them.

—Richard Branson

History is filled with people who have achieved extraordinary success.

Leonardo was an architect, astronomer, chemist, engineer, geologist, mathematician, inventor, physicist, and sculptor.

Aristotle was a logician, musician, philosopher, physicist, poet, politician, and zoologist.

Hildegard von Bingen was an author, artist, botanist, composer, linguist, medical researcher, poet, and theologian.

And yet, these people were mere mortals, just like you and me. The difference is that they set challenging goals and then seized the opportunity to rise to that challenge.

Don't shy away from daunting tasks, intimidating obstacles, or grand goals. Why shouldn't *you* achieve noteworthy success?

> *Today we grow gigantic arms that build in a month the pyramids that once consumed a million men; we make for ourselves great eyes that search out the invisible stars of the sky, and little eyes that peer into the invisible cells of life; we speak, if we wish, with quiet voices that reach across continents and seas; and we move over the land and the air with the freedom of timeless gods.*

—Will Durant

We humans have done some extraordinary things in the short time we have lived on this planet, and every one of us alive today should be inspired by these astounding accomplishments.

But we should also acknowledge that the men and women behind great achievements are fundamentally no different from you or me. For we *all* are born naked, helpless, human, into a strange and unknown world. And while our starting places may differ, history tells us that it is *possible* to rise from the bottom, right to the very top.

In your goal setting, don't be afraid to dream bigger, aim higher, and be bolder. Don't be afraid to set grand, ambitious, audacious goals.

You can go in life as far as you desire to go. But if you're not thinking big, you won't get anywhere near what you're capable of.

Planning Is Paramount

In preparing for battle, I have always found that plans are useless but planning is indispensable.

—Dwight D. Eisenhower

Despite what some Wall Street analysts may lead you to believe, it is impossible to predict what will happen, which is why there can never be a perfect plan. But you don't need a perfect plan, because the value of a plan is not in the plan itself; it's in what the plan does for you.

Planning forces you to think about what may or may not happen, lending you an advantage as events unfold in time.

Planning encourages you to take those first steps—always the hardest steps—and begin working toward your goals.

And planning inspires you to persist despite adversity, by reminding you of the prize that awaits you at the end.

Even though life won't go to plan, if you want to be successful, planning is essential.

You typically only see, experience, and get what you look for.

—Darren Hardy

Ever notice how, after finding a car you like online or on the sales floor, you begin seeing that same car everywhere you go? That's your reticular activating system, your RAS. (Remember, from Pillar 1?) And it's what makes planning so powerful.

When you plan, you begin thinking about what you want to accomplish and how you will do it. As your mind focuses on these things, your RAS starts scanning the world, looking for ways to get them—looking for ways to achieve your goals.

What a nice surprise: a computer in our mind with the sole purpose of helping us get to where we want to go. And yet, so many of us don't use it!

There will be plenty of obstacles to overcome before you reach your destination. Why not make use of all the tools you have at your disposal? Why not leverage your RAS? It's as simple as creating a plan.

> **It is better to have a bad plan than no plan.**
>
> **—Garry Kasparov**

It is a little ironic: We plan our vacations months, even years, in advance, right down to the teensiest detail. We plan our wardrobe—the number of skirts or shirts we need, their style, color, and size. And we plan our social lives. But when it comes to our dreams, our goals, and our life, we forget to plan.

That's why so many people drift along through life. They flow wherever the current takes them. It's possible that they end up on the white sandy beaches of health, wealth, and happiness. But it's also unlikely. More probably, they will strike land at destinations far less pleasant: the islands of debt, despair, and regret. But it doesn't have to be this way.

If you want more control over where you will end up one, two, or five years from today, then start making some plans for your life. Start living your life with intention.

Even a bad plan is better than no plan. For when you have a plan—any plan—you are at least aware of the destination you seek.

In five years' time, where will you be?

You need to plan the way a fire department plans. It cannot anticipate fires, so it has to shape a flexible organization that is capable of responding to unpredictable events.

—Andy Grove

The world is changing today faster than ever before in history, but that doesn't mean planning is pointless. All it means is that a static plan is not a sound plan. So what makes a sound plan? Five elements:

1. A sound plan is *simple*. One page is usually sufficient. How can you distill yours down?

2. A sound plan is *clear*. What do you want to achieve? And for you to achieve it, who needs to do what, by when, and how?

3. A sound plan is *creative*. What resources are at your disposal? How can you best deploy them?

4. A sound plan is *motivating*. What is the reward that awaits you? What is the price of failure?

5. A sound plan is *flexible*. If previously unknown information comes to light, how can you adjust to accommodate it?

Simple, clear, creative, motivating, flexible: the five elements of a sound plan.

No Action, No Success

Being able to execute is a special and distinct skill. It means a person knows how to put decisions into action and push them forward to completion, through resistance, chaos, or unexpected obstacles. People who can execute know that winning is about results.

—Jack Welch

All great achievements are born in the mind. But the dream alone, the idea alone, the plan alone—no matter how brilliant—is not enough.

That's why the most successful among us are often not the smartest. Rather, they are the ones who can push past the chaos of life and drive their goals and ambitions to completion. That is, the most successful among us are the ones who can *execute*.

So dream, but don't just be a dreamer. Think, but don't just be a thinker. Plan, but don't just be a planner. Results are what count, and they are possible only through *execution*.

Plans are only good intentions unless they immediately degenerate into hard work.

—Peter F. Drucker

Everything we do falls into one of three categories, three "buckets":

1. reflecting on the past,
2. executing in the present, or
3. planning for the future.

Goals can be achieved without reflecting and planning (although it's a lot tougher). But it's *impossible* to achieve our goals without executing.

So look back on your past and all that you have learned, look forward to your future and all that awaits you, then—and this is vital—come back to the *present* and take action.

Only by taking action in the present can you grow, change, and transform your life.

> *We must not confuse the present with the past. With regard to the past, no further action is possible.*
>
> **—Simone de Beauvoir**

Let the past teach you, and the future entice you, but be careful not to live too much of your life in either of these purely mind-induced states.

For although the past can educate, it can also weigh you down. And while the future can inspire you, it can also distract you. But more importantly, the only way you can achieve your goals is through taking action—*right now.*

So act! And if you fail, learn from that experience, pick yourself up, and then take more action! Dive headfirst into the pool of life! Grab the world with both hands! Choose to participate in this extraordinary existence!

Dreams may be the seedlings of reality, but they are not reality. Action creates the difference.

> *Begin doing what you want to do now. We are not living in eternity. We have only this moment, sparkling like a star in our hand—and melting like a snowflake.*
>
> **—Francis Bacon**

All that exists, all that you have to work with, is this present moment. Everything else is simply projections in your mind. That's why we must train ourselves to take action right now—to master that pesky devil procrastination.

How many times have you felt inspired to do something—enroll in an online course, learn to play a musical instrument, revamp your website, get a gym membership—only to lose the feeling, not take up the new task, then recall your inspiration months later, with nothing but regret to show?

Act before the feeling of inspiration passes. Act before the idea is lost amid the distractions of the mind and the moment. Act before your good intentions lose their potency.

The conditions for beginning will never be perfect. If you're waiting for the perfect situation, you could be waiting forever.

Executing Isn't Easy

The greatest man of action is he who is the greatest, and a life-long, dreamer. For in him the dreamer is fortified against destruction by a far-seeing eye, a virile mind, a strong will, a robust courage.

—Louis H. Sullivan

As you pursue your goals, you will encounter challenges great and small. The real challenge of success is learning to overcome these often unforeseen obstacles: to meet with and push past failure, keep going despite adversity, and bounce back from defeat stronger and with more ambition than before.

Getting over new and unplanned hurdles is never easy, but it's always possible. The key is to see the future you are creating, and to let it *pull* you through the challenges. Look for the light at the end of the tunnel. It may be only a tiny pinprick, but it's there.

Compared to the sun, Earth is a mere blip. The ant, beside the antelope, is a mere nothing. And the obstacles before you pale in comparison with the power of your dreams.

You can have anything you want—if you want it badly enough. You can be anything you want to be, have anything you desire, accomplish anything you set out to accomplish—if you will hold to that desire with single-ness of purpose.

—Robert Collier

You can achieve whatever you desire—if you *truly* desire it.

But don't mistake desire for a hope, a wish, or a craving. Desire is a powerful, consuming, enduring emotion that you feel through your entire body. When you desire something, you can hardly get it off your mind—and even then, not for long.

Desire is what drove Michelangelo to finish his Sistine Chapel masterpiece, Cornelius Vanderbilt to build his railroad empire, and Abraham Lincoln to spearhead the abolition of slavery in the United States.

The trouble that many people face is that they want success, but they don't *desire* it. And so, instead of working on their dreams, they do something easier—such as watching TV.

It will take hard work. Tears will flow. And you will sweat—figuratively and literally. But with desire to drive you, you can overcome anything that awaits.

What do you *truly* desire?

> *Somebody said that it couldn't be done*
>> *But he with a chuckle replied*
> *That "maybe it couldn't," but he would be one*
>> *Who wouldn't say no till he'd tried.*
> *So he buckled right in with the trace of a grin*
>> *On his face. If he worried he hid it.*
> *He started to sing as he tackled the thing*
>> *That couldn't be done, and he did it!*

—Edgar A. Guest

History is a repeating chronicle of human beings pushing boundaries and doing what others "knew" to be impossible. But what enables these men and women to overcome seemingly insurmountable odds?

The first part, clearly, is that they actually *begin*. (We both know, that's harder than it sounds.) But then what do these extraordinary people do? What's their secret? Simply this: After they begin, they *persist*.

All those who overcome great challenges do so simply by persisting. Why is persistence so powerful? Because small, seemingly insignificant steps, repeated consistently over time, can result in massive change. That's how the Great Wall of China got built: stone by stone, brick by brick.

No matter what lies in front of you, persist toward your destination. That might mean taking a different path from the one you first imagined. But as long as you keep heading toward your chosen port of call, eventually you will make it there.

The "little" things add up.

> *Be prepared for rejection. No matter how bad it is, don't let it overcome you and influence you—keep on going towards what you want to do—no matter what . . . You need to be as enthusiastic about door number one-hundred as door number one.*
>
> **—John Paul DeJoria**

If you truly desire to be successful, there is a word you had better get used to. It's not a particularly impressive word. It's not showy or swish. But it can stop you cold if you let it.

No. I'm busy.

No. We went with someone else.

No. That's too risky.

No. You're not smart enough.

Get used to *no*. Become friends with *no*. *No* will be around for the foreseeable future. It isn't going anywhere. And neither are you if you aren't prepared to face rejection. For there is not one single story of success that didn't have an intimate relationship with *no*.

Every rejection is an opportunity to learn. And everything learned is a step toward your dreams. So when *no* shows itself, politely acknowledge its presence, and then—within the bounds of law and conscience—push ever forward.

Blessings may appear under the shape of pains, losses, and disappointments; but let him have patience, and he will see them in their proper figures.

—**Joseph Addison**

Patience can be puzzling. We need it, but there's no formula telling us exactly how much is right. There's no line delineating between taking rash action and being too slow out of the blocks.

What *is* clear is that impatience is one of success's worst enemies, and one of failure's dearest companions. So as you raise your ambitions and work toward your goals, remember to be patient with yourself.

The good things in life take time: No meaningful relationship blossoms overnight. Valuable skills aren't mastered in a week. And beneficial habits aren't ingrained over a single month.

Life can sometimes be excruciatingly slow. And it can also be just plain old excruciating. A little patience can go a long way.

We are what we repeatedly do. Excellence, then, is not an act, but a habit . . . It is easy to perform a good action, but not easy to acquire a settled habit of performing such actions.

—**Will Durant**

A tapestry of positive habits is essential to executing your goals. But there are traps to be aware of. Habits cut both ways, which makes them a divisive topic.

On the one hand, as some spiritual teachers have argued, habits are unconscious, unenlightened acts that cause us to miss the essence of life. On the other hand, as Will Durant maintains, habits are the foundation that excellence is built on.

Who to believe? As always, you should draw your own conclusions. But perhaps you will consider this: strive to develop good habits, but at the same time, resist habituation. That means instilling the routines conducive to creating and living the life that you desire, while, in everything you do, trying to be present and mindful.

The Sunday morning run is far easier when you've been doing it every week for the past year. But don't miss the crisp, clean air; the magnificence of a simple, drooped leaf; or the radiant sunbeams dancing upon rooftops.

Commitment is doing the thing you said you would do, long after the mood you said it in has left you.

—Darren Hardy

When we first set goals and create plans, it's easy to feel inspired, motivated, and energized. What's far more challenging is sticking to the plan when we are tired, discouraged, or just don't feel like it.

You know the drill: You see the fitness magazine model with the six-pack abs and perfectly toned biceps, and you're inspired! You tell yourself, *I'm getting into shape. No more junk food. Gym two—no, three—times a week. I've put this off for too long!* Then . . . nothing.

Here's the reality: You're either committed and moving toward your goals, or uncommitted and moving away. You're either in the process of becoming who you desire to become, or in the process of becoming someone else.

Achieving goals takes sustained action—through the good times and the challenging times. Nothing less will get it done.

Everybody has a plan—until they get hit.

—Mike Tyson

There's one to your left. Another to your right. There's one above you, and another straight in front of you. What are they? Obstacles.

Some obstacles we expect, but many times they appear haphazardly, as if out of thin air. And to get past them, we need problem-solving skills.

As a simple approach to problem solving, try the following sequence of questions:

1. What is the problem? (Write it down concisely.)

2. What can *you* do to solve this problem?

3. If you can't solve the problem right now, what could you read that might help you?

4. After some research, if you still can't solve the problem, who could you ask for help?

You will be amazed at the problems you can solve by yourself. And also at the people—some of them perfect strangers—who are willing to help once they see that you are determined and have already taken the first steps.

Problem solving: a life skill.

Each of us must choose to suffer one of two pains: the pain of discipline or the pain of regret.

—Jim Rohn

One of the greatest temptations in life is to ease up a little and let all that hard-won self-discipline slide. The problem is that even the smallest neglect or lack of self-discipline grows and spreads like an infection into the rest of our actions.

That doesn't mean we shouldn't take a well-earned break from our goals and ambitions. Indeed, we must, for success requires balance. And if we are confident in our ambition, we know that it will still be there when we return, refreshed and reenergized, from our holiday.

The point is that life is a choice between a little pain now and a lot of pain later. There's the pain of setting goals, making plans, and executing. The pain of going to the gym, tackling a difficult course of study, or writing a personal letter. Then there's the pain of meandering through life with no clear direction and ending up with poor health, limited education, and conflict-ridden relationships.

The price of self-discipline is always less than the price of regret. It's small, positive decisions, made consistently over time, that lead to great achievement.

And so . . .

You can't work everything out at the start. That's just not the way life works. A major part of the adventure is simply learning more about yourself—about what fulfils you, what inspires you, what motivates you. Happily, we don't need all the answers. All we need is a refinement in our philosophy so that we walk a well-thought-out path through life.

What does such a path look like? It varies, of course. But it always includes the combination of effective and efficient action. Effective action means *doing the right things*, which we can do only if we have wise goals. And efficient action means *doing things right*, which we can do only if we have sound plans.

We touched earlier on the simplified formula for success. Here's the long version:

1. Devote the introspection required to find out what truly matters to you.

2. Using that information, set yourself short- and long-term goals in each of the many arenas of life.

3. Revise those goals, aiming far higher than you think you could ever hit.

4. Make sound plans.

5. Take action.

6. One by one, surmount the obstacles.

7. Refine as required.

Dreams, goals, and plans exist to serve you in life—to help you achieve all that you could ever want. If you don't already make use of these vital tools, maybe today is the day to begin. Maybe the time is right now.

Understand "Success" and "Failure"

What Is Success, Really?

Success Must Be Earned

Prime Your Mind for Success

Failure Is Unavoidable; Failing Intelligently Is Not

MUCH OF OUR lives is determined by our philosophy. And a core component of that philosophy is a sound understanding of, and appreciation for, success and failure.

Success means creating and living the best life we can, which comes of setting wise goals and being self-disciplined enough to go after them every day. While success is relatively simple, it isn't easy. What this means is that success won't be handed to us—we must earn it.

Understanding that we earn our accomplishments is one part of "priming our minds" for success. Another part is the recognition that to succeed, we must become the masters of our minds. That means learning how to focus our energy and developing a deep understanding of ourselves—who we are, what we value, what we're passionate about, and how we operate.

We must also give ourselves permission to fail. It is worth reiterating, again and again, that failure is part of success. Every world-class athlete, brilliant entrepreneur, or groundbreaking scientist faced dozens, perhaps hundreds or thousands, of failures before succeeding.

That's because failure is opportunity in disguise. For when we fail, we are presented with a chance to learn the lessons we need to learn in order to achieve the success we desire. It is through our failures that we earn our right to succeed—so long as we are failing intelligently.

From La Rinconada in the Peruvian Andes (the world's highest-elevation human habitation) to McMurdo Station in Antarctica (the southernmost), to China's Motuo County, which is inaccessible by automobile, success means different things to different people at different times. Find out what it means to you, and leverage your failures to help you get there.

What Is Success, Really?

For me success was always going to be a Lamborghini.
But now I've got it, it just sits on my drive.

—Curtis Jackson ("50 Cent")

At first, we all tend to share the same popular notion of success: material wealth, objects, fame. But then we change. Maybe we acquire what we desired, and it doesn't fulfill us the way we imagined it would. Or something else comes along—say, our life partner, children, or a spiritual awakening—which proves far more precious than anything we could have wished for. And we are amazed at how naive we were.

Real success is less about public adoration and more about private respect—the respect of friends and family. It is less about material fortune and more about the priceless treasure of knowing the depths of your heart, soul, and mind. And it is less about showboating and more about deep, humble self-confidence.

Don't be confused by the many mirages of success. Make sure you are chasing what is real.

I have known millionaires starving for lack of the nutriment which alone can sustain all that is human in man, and I know workmen, and many so-called poor men, who revel in luxuries beyond the power of those millionaires to reach . . . There is no class so pitiably wretched as that which possesses money and nothing else.

—Andrew Carnegie

The great debate: does wealth increase happiness? To an extent, yes, it can help a great deal. This you already know from your own experience. But there's more to it.

While wealth is unlikely to make you miserable, no amount of money, no make of car, no size of house, no exotic overseas ski adventure will make you truly fulfilled. Amassing a great fortune does not guarantee you a contented life. Far more important than material fortune are relationships, freedom, and health.

The complication is that many of us are terrible at accurately determining what will fulfill us. That's because we tend to confuse our desire for a core human need, such as freedom, with an object that might provide it, such as a car.

The key to avoiding that trap is to project your life forward to the point where you have attained the object you desire, and then try to determine the impact it will have on you. How much better will your life really be?

While material possessions can indicate success, they themselves are not success.

Money is a new form of slavery, and distinguishable from the old simply by the fact that it is impersonal— that there is no human relation between master and slave.

—Leo Tolstoy

Wealth can be a great motivator. Its allure can inspire us to dedicate our lives to a cause and make a contribution to the world that we wouldn't otherwise have made. But an *obsession* for money is counterproductive to a successful life. For even though money can enable us to do great and wonderful things, its single-minded pursuit will rob us of our serenity, and perhaps even our family and friends.

Poor indeed are those who live for money and nothing else. Their stock portfolios and bank accounts may be full, but their souls are empty, their hearts unfulfilled.

Do what you can, with what you've got, where you are.

—Squire Bill Widener

We've covered what success isn't. It isn't fame, fortune, or any sort of material possession. So, what is it?

Technically speaking, success is the accomplishment of something that you set out to accomplish. Following this, you could be "successful" with a job application or your goal to climb Mt. Everest. But this is a very narrow definition. And it isn't the success we are discussing.

The success we are discussing is the *ultimate* success. It means being able to leave this life with contentment when death eventually comes. And it comes of creating and living the best life you can: giving everything you have and making the most of your limited time on this planet.

Underpinning this broad definition are four elements that characterize success. (For further discussion, see appendix 1.) Of these elements, the most important one to understand is that success is *relative*: relative to the circumstances of your birth and relative to what you want to do while blood and oxygen still circulate through your body.

That's why success for you is different from success for anyone else. And also why it's impossible to be successful if you haven't established what success means for *you*.

So find out how you want to spend your limited time on this planet. Find out what motivates you, energizes you, inspires you, and fulfills you. And once you know this, make it your focus. Defend your dreams against any erosive influence, be it friends, family, or society. Stand resolute on what is important to you. And strive every day toward creating and living the life you desire.

Genuine success is to live a balanced life, to have happiness, health and prosperity.

—James Breckenridge Jones

What if you had a stock portfolio worth hundreds of millions of dollars? Sounds pretty good, right? But what if that meant you could never see your spouse, children, or best friend ever again?

Or say you had your own ski chalet at Courchevel 1850 in France. There you could dine at Hôtel Le Chabichou or Le Bateau Ivre—both Michelin many-starred restaurants. Amazing, yes? Well, not if you're so unhealthy that your body can't handle the thin air at six thousand feet, which is the altitude of the village center.

Success is ultimately about living a balanced life—balanced in health, wealth, relationships, and spirituality. And even if you don't value all these things right now, experience suggests—anecdotally but emphatically—that you will value them at some stage of your life.

But let's be clear: balance doesn't mean you have to be in a state of perfect equilibrium all the time—you wouldn't be able to move! And life simply can't be ordered that precisely. So some months, even years, might have a little heavier (or lighter) workload than others. But if we desire to be successful, our lives *must* eventually reach a balanced state.

Creating and maintaining that balance won't be easy. Beware of becoming so focused, so single minded, in achieving your goals that you overemphasize one part of your life and neglect others. And especially don't mistreat your relationships—they are far more valuable than anything money can buy.

Success Must Be Earned

If you can fill the unforgiving minute

With sixty seconds worth of distance run,

Yours is the Earth and everything that's in it . . .

—Rudyard Kipling

Successful and unsuccessful people have the same twenty-four hours in the day. The difference lies in how they use those hours.

How do you spend your days? Do you make the most of each minute? Do you get *from* the day and not just *through* it? If you're like most people, probably not.

To be sure, we have ample excuses available to explain away our neglect. After a long day's work, we're tired. And we have cooking to do, bills to pay, children to help with their homework, and the big game to watch on TV. There's just not enough time to do it all. But there *is* enough time—we just happen to be highly skilled at letting it slip through our fingers.

Try to make the most of every moment. Spend your time productively, on things that matter—on things that move you toward the life you desire.

You earn success by making the most of your time.

Resolve to pay the price to succeed. For everything we want in life, there is a price. Success comes only after you've paid the price, never before.

—Brian Tracy

Everything in life, including success, has a price. The problem is that most people like the idea of being successful, but they're not willing to do what it takes to get there.

Success doesn't happen overnight. We achieve it incrementally over time, through daily self-discipline that consistently inches us toward our goals. And long before the benefits of success begin to accrue, someone has been quietly cultivating the ground: with a sound philosophy, a set of relevant skills, and an arsenal of positive habits.

How badly do you want it? What price are you willing to pay? Would you dare turn off the TV in the middle of your favorite show?

Success comes at a price. Often, that price is convenience.

> *Nothing is given to you. Whatever you do, you've got to work for it and earn it. Whatever reward you get you've got to know that you've had your input into that success. There's no substitute for hard work.*
>
> **—Jack Charlton**

If we want to live better lives tomorrow, we sometimes have to do things we don't want to do today. For there is typically a gap between our dreams and our reality, and closing it involves both pain and arduous effort.

Welcome the pain and sweat. No, they aren't pleasant, but it is through difficulty that we grow, and pain signals us that something is wrong, thereby bringing to our attention the areas in life where we need to improve.

It's also worth remembering that hard work can be enjoyable, especially if you can keep your eyes on the prize. That's because big achievements happen one small step at a time. And one of life's great thrills is to edge ever closer toward the life of our dreams.

Success comes through hard work, but hard work doesn't have to be *hard*.

The big secret in life is, there is no secret. Whatever your goal, you can get there—as long as you're willing to work.

—Oprah Winfrey

Hard work is necessary—you can't get there without it. But it doesn't *guarantee* success. All it gets you is a ticket to the game. You can be honest, sincere, helpful, and hardworking your entire life and still end up far from where you wanted to be.

To succeed, you have to be more than a hard worker. You have to be a *smart* worker. That means working on yourself—refining your philosophy, improving your attitude, developing new skills, and cultivating positive habits—so that you become someone who has *earned* success.

Work on *you*. It's the quickest path to your dreams.

Opportunity is missed by most people because it is dressed in overalls and looks like work.

—Thomas Edison

People often confuse success with opportunity: they suppose that successful people got that way because the opportunities landed in their lap.

Don't be confused by opportunity. It is not the thing you want, tied with a nice bow and handed to you while you lie in a hammock. Opportunity is a *set of circumstances* that makes it possible for you to achieve a desirable outcome. It could be a networking event, a position opening up in a different division of your company, or a book recommended by a friend. Opportunities come to all of us, but only those who take advantage of them as they arise will benefit.

That's why *you* are the key ingredient in opportunity. For it is up to you to recognize when an opportunity arises; and it is up to you to take advantage of that.

You earn success by being prepared when opportunity comes knocking.

> *For 12 years, I listened to a tape of my own voice every single night before I went to sleep. I was talking directly to my subconscious and I played the tape when my mind was most receptive. My income doubled for three years in a row . . . I have to say that this is the most powerful thing I've done to climb out of my blue-collar upbringing.*
>
> **—Chet Holmes**

The external signs of success are reflections of an inner environment refined long before success arrived. They are also a testament to the many obstacles overcome on the journey. People don't always understand this, because it's far easier to see the results of success than to see the foundations laid, or the challenges met, to get those results.

Here's the question: Are you prepared to do what it takes to be successful? Will you devote the time to cultivate an inner environment that enables you to succeed? And will you persevere through the many obstacles that will push you to the brink of failure?

Unless you lay the foundations that success requires, and surmount the inevitable obstacles that will arise on the journey, success won't come.

Most people like the idea of success—just not enough to do what it requires of them.

Prime Your Mind for Success

A man who acquires the ability to take full possession of his own mind may take possession of anything else to which he is justly entitled.

—Andrew Carnegie

Many people have poor control over their minds. They can't focus their efforts where they would like to. Even when they know they should be working, they can't keep from being distracted. And not coincidentally, many people aren't successful.

Start working on your ability to stay focused on where you are and what you are doing. Focused concentration is a learnable skill, and it can become a habit, but only if you practice every day. It's a simple as this: whatever you are doing, *do that*.

Once you have learned this skill, your mind ceases being yet another obstacle to overcome, and starts working for you to achieve your goals. And doesn't *that* sound nice!

Take full control of your mind, and you will have full control of your life.

Thinking is the hardest work there is, which is probably the reason so few engage in it.

—Henry Ford

The world has many hard workers, but far fewer hard thinkers. Perhaps for this reason, there are many stories of average achievement, and far fewer of exceptional achievement.

Strive to become a good *thinker*. It isn't difficult. It's just that most of us haven't learned how to think properly, and most of us don't make time for thinking.

Good thinking begins with taking stock. What kinds of information are you letting into your mind, and what kinds of thoughts are arising there? Your mind is like a factory: It can't put out a quality product if the raw material is inferior. So make sure the information you are absorbing, and the thoughts you are having, are steering you toward a life of confidence and boldness, not fear and timidity.

After you have appraised the raw material, then you determine what to do with what you have. It's a three-part process:

1. Ponder your past and all that you have learned.

2. Dream of your future and all that you desire.

3. Look hard at the present and decide how best to deploy your time and energy.

Success arises from ideas that form in your mind, born of the information you gather, processed through the thinking habits you cultivate. Don't just think—think smart.

> *It is what you read when you don't have to that determines what you will be when you can't help it.*
>
> **—Oscar Wilde**

Being proactive means taking action now so you can better control a situation that is coming. It is a common trait among the successful because it enables you to mold the future to your advantage.

On top of that, being proactive prepares you ahead of time to take advantage of opportunity when it inevitably presents itself. For opportunity is not a matter of *if*. It is always a matter of *when*. And only those who are ready to seize opportunity when it appears will benefit from it.

So start reading the books, developing your skills, and cultivating your self-discipline. Then, when the window of opportunity opens, you will be ready.

> *Only as you do know yourself can your brain serve you as a sharp and efficient tool.*
>
> **—Bernard M. Baruch**

Success stems from effectiveness and efficiency—the ability to do the right things in the right way. The trouble for many people is that they don't know themselves well enough to know what the right things are, or how to do them in the right way. That's why developing the skills of self-direction and self-awareness is so important.

Self-direction is knowing where you want to go. It begins with the understanding that you alone are the captain of your ship and the master of your destiny.

Self-awareness is understanding how you operate. It means knowing what works for you and what works against you, what drives you and what tempts you, and when and how you do your best work.

Doing the right things in the right way is the quickest path to success. But that path is open only to those who know (1) where they want to go, and (2) how they operate best. Are you clear on those two things?

> *People often say that motivation doesn't last. Well, neither does bathing. That's why we recommend it daily.*
>
> **—Zig Ziglar**

Look around you, and you will find many examples of wonderfully talented people who failed, just as you can find plenty of supposedly ordinary people who achieved extraordinary success.

That's because talent is but one small part of success. Far more important, and often unobserved, are the driving motivations behind our successes. The issue is, true motivation exists in only one place in all the world: inside you. And the only person with the key, the combination, the access code, is *you*. No one else can light that fire.

If you haven't found your fire yet, spend more time looking inside. What gets you excited? What are you passionate about? What is your mind naturally drawn to?

When you love something, the problem is how to switch your motivation *off*, not on. So get the necessary information to understand your desires and ambitions, and then watch as your motivation—and success—grows like never before.

The pursuit of your dreams is the most surefire alarm clock in the world. And it doesn't have a snooze button.

Success is stumbling from failure to failure with no loss of enthusiasm.

—Unknown

The way we feel reflects in the way we think. And the way we think influences how we act. So we find, unsurprisingly, that our feelings affect our actions. (Who would have thought?)

The predicament is that negative emotions are part and parcel of failure, and failure is an equally essential component of success. Thus, mishandling our failures can diminish our ambition, mask our motivation, dampen our enthusiasm, and *rob* us of success.

Don't let your failures derail you. Learn how to manage the emotional roller coaster that is the road to success. The key is to prepare yourself mentally for some of the more formidable emotions you are bound to face on your journey. Doubt, fear, confusion, disappointment, stress, anxiety—they're going to come up, so don't be surprised when they do.

Be wise enough to look down the road. And if you see storm clouds, pack a raincoat.

Failure Is Unavoidable; Failing Intelligently Is Not

I've missed more than 9,000 shots in my career. I've lost almost 300 games. Twenty-six times, I've been trusted to take the game-winning shot and missed. I've failed over and over and over again in my life. And that is why I succeed.

—Michael Jordan

Mention the word "failure" and see the faces of those around you react as if it were a contagious disease. The irony is, the greatest achievers are often the ones who have failed the *most*.

Statistically, that makes a lot of sense. The only way to rise to the top of any field is by spending countless hours honing your craft. And the more time you spend, the more opportunity you have to fail. So get used to it (but not *too* used to it).

People who rise to the top also surround themselves with others who are as good as—or better than—they are. For that's how you learn the fastest. And it's also how you end up failing a lot. (Starting to notice the correlation?)

Next time you find yourself worrying about failure, remember that the greatest achievers are not those who fail the least; they are the ones *least frightened* of failure. If you're failing—and learning from your failures—you are moving toward success.

It is fine to celebrate success, but it is more important to heed the lessons of failure.

—Bill Gates

Your failures present you with opportunities to learn and grow. Thus, they can be stepping-stones toward success.

The dilemma is that the introspection required to assess our failures objectively and figure out the role that we ourselves played can be painful. That's why so many of us don't transform our failures into opportunities.

As painful as it may be, we must ask ourselves: What role did I play in this failed situation? What could I have done differently? What can I take from this and apply moving forward in my life?

Take the time to review your failures and extract the lessons from them. This is how you transform negative into positive. And it's how you succeed.

Fail, or fail and learn. It's your choice.

My great concern is not whether you have failed, but whether you are content with your failure.

—Abraham Lincoln

We all will face obstacles, challenges, setbacks, and failures on our journey. And the unfortunate reality is that many of us give up just as we are on the verge of reaching our goals.

Don't let that be your story. Be one of the brave few who refuse to quit, who never give in, who keep on going until they achieve their goals. Success *is* possible for you, but only if you are willing to repeatedly meet with, and push past, failure.

The trick is in making your failures work for you, not against you. And that you can do by choosing to be discontented, disappointed, and unsatisfied with failure. In doing so, you leverage those powerful emotions to help you rise above your current situation and continue on your journey.

Learning from failure is only the first half of failing intelligently. The other half is harnessing the powerful emotions that accompany failure, and using them to energize, motivate, and propel you forward.

Right here is the point at which the majority of men meet with failure, because of their lack of persistence in creating new plans to take the place of those which fail . . . Remember when your plans fail, that temporary defeat is not permanent failure . . . Temporary defeat should mean only one thing, the certain knowledge that there is something wrong with your plan.

—Napoleon Hill

In pursuing your goals, you always have three paths available to you. Understanding these paths is the key to understanding failure.

The first path is the *path ahead*. To walk this path means to keep marching directly forward. When an obstacle arises and it knocks you down, you pick yourself up, figure out what happened, and go through or over that obstacle the next time. It might take longer than expected, but you reach your destination with only minor course corrections.

That's the path Thomas Edison chose. The man who gave us the incandescent lightbulb failed thousands of times before he accomplished his goal. But to him, he wasn't failing. Every wrong attempt was a learning opportunity—and, hence, a step closer to his goal.

The second path is the *path around*. Those who take this path know where they want to go, but they keep hitting a roadblock that's had them stuck for a while. So what do they do? They gather all they have learned, and then find a new route to take them to their target.

Dwayne "the Rock" Johnson chose this path. At age 24, with just seven dollars to his name, and a track record of failure in both the NFL and the Canadian Football League, he started training for wrestling. And the rest is history.

The third and final path is the *path to nowhere*. This is the path walked by those who fall short of their goals and give up, failing to recognize that success is still achievable if they would only learn from their mistakes and continue toward their destination—through or around whatever is in their way.

Unfortunately, this path is far and away the most popular one, but not by choice. People rarely *choose* this path. They wander onto it unknowingly—and often never get off it. You personally know many people who have walked it. *You* have walked it. *I* have walked it. We *all* have walked it. And you may remember, as I do, that distinctly funereal feel: the death of a dream.

So go onward. Or go around. But don't go *nowhere*. Learn from your failures. Better yet, leverage them to drive you forward. Failure is unavoidable, but failing intelligently is not.

And so . . .

Success is not fame. And it isn't material possessions or wealth (though they often accompany it). Success means creating and living the best life you can, during that finite time when you have the gift of being able to draw breath. It is the ultimate accomplishment, and it comes of knowing what matters to you, and making that the focus of your life.

That's the first half of the story. For we cannot discuss success without discussing failure. Indeed, the opportunity to succeed is always accompanied by the possibility of failure. And as we climb to ever greater heights, the distance between us and the ground also grows.

What's more, it is by the sting of failure itself that we enable ourselves to succeed. For failure is a harsh but effective teacher—a bringer of both pain and opportunity in equal measure—who can lead us toward success if we are wise enough to listen.

But be careful, for even though success is the golden child, and failure is opportunity in disguise, both have their traps. Too often, with success comes arrogance and lack of balance. And with failure comes timidity and lack of ambition.

So learn from failure, but don't dwell on it. And celebrate success, but don't lose sight of the fundamentals that enabled it to happen.

Embrace Change and Take Risks

Change Begins with Awareness

Inside, Then Outside; Your World, Then *the* World

Be a Shrewd Risk Taker

The Greatest Risks

Dealing with Fear and Risk Aversion

To ACHIEVE ALL that we are capable of, we must welcome change. And, like it or not, we must take risks.

The process of changing ourselves requires that we become aware of the need for change, recognize and overcome our inherent resistance to change, and understand that if we change what is on the inside, change will then manifest for us on the outside.

We cannot avoid risk in life. In fact, life began for us with the huge, audacious risk of leaving the security of the womb for a bright, noisy, scary world. Still, we can minimize risk, and we can seek to take the right *kinds* of risks: the ones that will allow us to truly live life—to grow, develop, and become all that we are capable of.

But with change and risk comes fear—fear of stepping into the unknown, of losing sight of the shore and leaving our comfort zone. That's why a major part of embracing change and taking risks is learning how to conquer fear.

Embracing change and taking risks isn't easy, but it is possible. And it's absolutely necessary for success.

Change Begins with Awareness

A year from now you may wish you had started today.

—Karen Lamb

When looking back on our lives, we often can see clearly the decisions we made (or avoided making) and their impact. It could be frivolous spending sprees, ongoing procrastination, or unhealthy eating habits, leaving us with big credit card bills, unfinished projects, or a body we don't feel good about.

Hold up. If we can see so clearly the impact of our decisions, why, then, do we struggle so to learn from the past? Why, then, do we have such difficulty understanding that it is our actions and decisions *today* that determine our future? Why, then, do we not change our lives?

Answer: because change is *hard*.

Anyone who tells you change is easy doesn't understand the complexity of change. But that complexity lies not in the act of change itself; it lies in developing the *awareness* that leads to change. Would you agree that it's easy to leave your house and go to the gym? You get up, go outside, then drive, walk, or take public transport. Anyone can do that. The hard part is being aware of the need to do so.

When you are aware of both the need to change and the benefits of change, you will make change happen.

To become different from what we are, we must have some awareness of what we are.

—Eric Hoffer

Sometimes it seems as if other people can change us. When someone belittles us, we start acting small. Or if someone showers us with praise, we strut around with an inflated ego.

What really happens is that we receive a message, we interpret that message, and then we act on that interpretation. In other words, our actions stem from our mind's interpretation of events. Thus, *we* are the determining factor.

That's why no one else can change us. Only we can change ourselves. The problem is that we usually can see the need for change in others but not in ourselves. And before change can come, *we* must see the need for it.

Begin by trying to see things as they are, as opposed to how you *think* they are. Are you truly happy with your life? Are you where you thought you would be by now? Are you doing what you want to be doing? If the answer is no, what does that mean?

A strong dose of reality helps you become aware of and accept the need to change. With that awareness and acceptance, you'll be ready to do what it takes.

Faced with the choice between changing one's mind and proving that there is no need to do so, almost everyone gets busy on the proof.

—John K. Galbraith

To embrace change, strive to develop an open, aware, and objective mind. Remove the obscured lens that hides your faults, and look plainly at *who you are*. That isn't easy. (After all, if change were easy, everyone would be doing it.) But it is possible.

The first step is to become aware that we all are inherently biased in how we view ourselves and the world. We see our merits but not our imperfections. And we welcome any information that confirms what we believe to be true, and ignore, misinterpret, or conveniently overlook anything that suggests otherwise.

This bias makes it difficult for us to appreciate the need for change in ourselves. And that's an issue because we will instigate change only when our own awareness compels us to.

Don't spend your energy on proving there is no problem. We all have problems. Spend it on raising your awareness and finding a solution.

> *We cannot change what we are not aware of, and once we are aware, we cannot help but change.*
>
> **—Sheryl Sandberg**

Change begins with awareness of our need for change and also of our inherent *resistance* to change.

An unfortunate reality of life is that most people change only when the pain of staying the same becomes greater than the pain of changing. It's an unfortunate reality because the technological advancements of the modern world have created an environment that can become a sort of limbo: a place where we can live moderately contented lives, with average happiness, in largely tolerable conditions.

The problem is that such an environment is not uncomfortable enough to motivate us to change. As a result, we hover in place, not losing altitude, but not gaining it, either; not regressing, but not moving forward. This is how many of us get stuck in middle management, with a mortgage and a maddening mind.

If you find yourself heading toward such a world (or perhaps realize you are in that world right now), here's some good news: You can avoid the pitfall and escape the trap. For when you become aware of this human tendency—our unwillingness to change until things get bad enough—you can take back the steering wheel and decide to kick-start the process of change in your life.

Change can start whenever you want it to.

Success in life requires overcoming one of the most powerful forces in human nature: the resistance to change. To succeed in this world, you have to change all the time.

—Sam Walton

Why are we all so stubbornly resistant to change? What is it about consistency that we find so reassuring and comforting? Don't we know that it is through change that all growth happens? Don't we understand that embracing change is one of the most powerful mind-sets we can cultivate?

The opportunities of today are more plentiful than ever before. We can travel with relative ease to the farthest reaches of the globe. We can take classes, for free, from Stanford, MIT, Princeton, and Harvard. And with a few hundred dollars, we can found a business capable of reaching almost half the world's seven billion people. The thing is, those who embrace change will be the ones who benefit most.

You can fight change (and pay the price) or embrace it and let change take you on an astounding journey. Success isn't being rationed. There's enough to go around for all of us.

It is not the most intellectual of the species that survives; it is not the strongest that survives; but the species that survives is the one that is able best to adapt and adjust to the changing environment in which it finds itself.

—Leon C. Megginson

There will always be people who are stronger, smarter, or more skilled than you are. But don't worry, because the key to success is adaptability—the ability to change yourself and thrive in whatever environment you are in.

This truth is most evident when we look at the evolution of species. Humans now are the dominant species on this planet. For better or worse, we are running the show. Why? For the sole reason that we have adapted well.

The power of adaptability (and the high cost of inflexibility) is also clear as we witness the disruption of multibillion-dollar industries all around the world. Take the movie-rental industry, where Netflix has displaced the once mighty Blockbuster; or newspapers, where traditional publishers (the historical power holders for centuries) are fighting for their very survival against new digital formats.

To thrive in life, we must be willing and able to adapt—to let go of who we are today so we can evolve into someone greater tomorrow.

Inside, Then Outside; Your World, Then *the* World

Don't try to change the seed, don't change the soil, don't change the sunshine, don't change the rain, don't change the mix of seasons . . . Start working on the inside: work on your philosophy, work on your attitude, work on your personality, work on your language, work on the gift of communication . . . If you'll start making those personal changes, I'm telling you everything will change for you.

—Jim Rohn

When we think of change, we often think of our external environment: the clothes we wear, the car we drive, the house we live in, the friends we see. But changes in our external environment are merely a reflection of change that has occurred *within* us. Long before our external environment alters, we have been transforming ourselves on the inside.

Before the money flows in, the successful businessperson has in mind the knowledge that will lead to success. *Before* the awards ceremony, the Olympic medalist has cultivated the self-discipline that made a podium finish possible. And *before* a relationship blossoms in harmony, the enlightened spouse has devoted the time and care to understand their partner.

If you want to change your life, don't try to change what's on the outside. Seek first to change what's on the inside. Seek first to change your philosophy.

We need to be the change we wish to see in the world.

—Arun Gandhi

What world do you dream of? Is it a world free from prejudice or violence? Perhaps it is a world where people have the courage to follow their dreams. Or a world where all nations and peoples coexist in harmony.

Whatever you dream, the first step toward making it a reality in *the* world is to make it a reality in *your* world. Start changing everything you need to change, to align your life with the world you dream. Then, as if by magic, the world will start changing around you.

We see this in nature: At dusk over Rome, hordes of starlings take to the skies. Thousands of birds stream and swirl together above the city. It is simultaneous chaos and order as the flock darts unpredictably this way and that.

One explanation for this behavior is that a few individual birds signal a change in direction, that signal travels through the entire flock, and the flock adjusts accordingly. In other words, change among many comes of change by a few.

If you want to change the world, begin by changing *your* world.

Be a Shrewd Risk Taker

All courses of action are risky, so prudence is not in avoiding danger (it's impossible), but calculating risk and acting decisively. Make mistakes of ambition and not mistakes of sloth. Develop the strength to do bold things, not the strength to suffer.

—Niccolò Machiavelli

Risk pervades the universe. Driving to work, going shopping, even walking the dog around the block—nothing we do comes risk free. But there are different types of risk, and often when we mitigate one, we expose ourselves to another.

In avoiding the risk of failure, you risk never growing. Protecting yourself from the risk of vulnerability, you risk never experiencing intimacy. And trying to shelter yourself from "too much" risk may leave you defenseless against the risk of regret.

You can't avoid risk in life. But you can learn to take the right kinds of risk—the kinds that lead you toward the life you desire.

Often the difference between a successful man and a failure is not one's better abilities or ideas, but the courage that one has to bet on his idea, to take a calculated risk—and to act.

—Maxwell Maltz

We all have talents and we all have ideas, but some of us choose not to employ those talents or act on those ideas. Why? Because it's risky.

What if it doesn't work out the way I planned?
What if I'm not good enough?
What if I embarrass myself?

There's some basis for that old sound track. Things could go wrong, you might not (yet) have the skills, and people could laugh at you. The problem is, these worries represent only one side of the story: the downside. And sadly, that's the side most people focus on.

When weighing up risk, remember to ask: What if things go to plan? What if I *am* good enough? What if I *do* succeed?

It's important to understand what might go wrong, but don't forget to compare the downside with the upside. Calculated risk taking is what leads to success.

> *This nation was built by men who took risks: pioneers who were not afraid of the wilderness, businessmen who were not afraid of failure, scientists who were not afraid of the truth, thinkers who were not afraid of progress, dreamers who were not afraid of action.*
>
> **—Brooks Atkinson**

The great nations of the world were founded on the actions of men and women who risked much—all the way back to 1.75 million years ago, when *Homo erectus* migrated out of Africa and into Eurasia. But it would be naive to think these men and women (and early hominids) didn't seek to mitigate the risk where they could.

Consider Captain James Cook, the famed British explorer who charted the east coast of Australia. He also led the first circumnavigation of the Earth in which no crew member was lost to scurvy.

When preparing for an expedition, he sought to nurture a culture among his crew that would protect them from the psychological risks of isolation. He also imposed stringent guidelines for cleanliness and diet, to reduce the likelihood of sickness at sea. In other words, the Captain understood the risks and tried to mitigate them as best he could.

To ignore risk is sheer foolhardiness. To understand and mitigate it is wisdom.

Progress always involves risk. You can't steal second and keep one foot on first base.

—Robert Quillen

We all take risks in life. While some risk more than others, the appropriate degree of risk is a question of temperament: Given our goals, ambitions, and current stage of life, how much risk are we comfortable with?

Still, it's important to understand the relationship between risk and reward: the greater the risk, the greater the potential reward. Conversely, if you are not willing to take any risks, you can't expect to reap any reward.

Great achievement requires great risk. There is no other way.

The person who risks nothing does nothing, has nothing, is nothing, and becomes nothing. He may avoid suffering and sorrow, but he simply cannot learn and feel and change and grow and love and live.

—Leo Buscaglia

With each experience in life come emotions. We could even say that life is simply us experiencing emotions on our journey. And the greater the breadth and depth of what we feel, the more we have lived.

But the emotional experience can be active or passive. We can seek to fashion a broad variety of experiences, or we can simply go with the flow. While going with the flow is easier, making our own waves and charting our own course will deliver far greater depth and diversity of emotion—in other words, more life.

That's where risk comes in, because taking risks can bring us some of the most powerful emotions we will ever experience. It is the narrow escape, the hard-fought win, the summoning of courage, that makes for some of our most memorable moments.

Living to your fullest in your relationships, career, and spiritual life is impossible without taking risks.

> *Take your risks now. As you grow older, you become more fearful and less flexible. And I mean that literally. I hurt my knee on the treadmill this week and it wasn't even on.*
>
> **—Amy Poehler**

The older we get, the more deeply we feel our roots buried in the ground. In our youth, we tend to think we have all the time in the world. Both these mind-sets provide a great excuse for us to put off what we should be doing, and avoid the risks we should be taking, to create the life of our dreams.

If you think you've left it too late or that you've got a few spare years to mess about, take another look at life. For even the longest life is brief. And you won't leave this planet with anything more than you arrived with, so don't get too attached to those possessions of yours.

There is nothing you can own forever, and you will depart this world far sooner than you think. It's never too late—or too early—to start chasing your dreams.

> *The choice is not between success and failure; it is between choosing risk and striving for greatness or risking nothing and being certain of mediocrity.*
>
> **—Keith Ferrazzi**

Most people are unwilling to risk what they have today for what they could have tomorrow. If this is a conscious decision based on their true degree of risk tolerance, then it's likely a wise decision, because risk is a matter of temperament. But more often than not, this isn't the case.

That's because most people haven't devoted the necessary introspection to determine what their degree of risk tolerance truly is. They don't know how much risk they can handle. And as a result, they end up taking far fewer risks than they might have wished they did.

The path of too little risk is the path of regret. It is also the path of the ordinary, average middle-of-the-roader. If you don't know how much risk you are comfortable with, now is probably a good time to find out. Ask yourself, what would I regret more: taking the risk and failing, or making no attempt?

The Greatest Risks

When you play it too safe, you're taking the biggest risk of your life.

—**Barbara Sher**

On a table in front of you are two bags. One bag holds in it discomfort that will leap out at you immediately. The other bag also holds discomfort, but that discomfort will not present itself for another five years. Which bag do you choose?

There is no right or wrong answer. There are consequences, though. If you choose the first bag, you face immediate discomfort, but you also have the opportunity to overcome that situation and *grow*. If, on the other hand, you choose the second bag, you have avoided discomfort for a while. But as it sat in the bag, it festered and grew into a different sort of discomfort, whose name is *Regret*. Those who choose the second bag will forever wonder what they missed out on by not confronting discomfort those five years earlier.

This is life's trade-off: a little discomfort now, or a lot of regret later. And whether you realize it or not, this trade-off is quietly going on all the time.

Taking too little risk is one of the greatest risks there is.

Twenty years from now you will be more disappointed by the things you didn't do than by the ones you did. So throw off the bowlines, sail away from the safe harbor, catch the trade winds in your sails. Explore. Dream. Discover.

—**H. Jackson Brown Jr.**

Here's the difference between young and old: the young think risk is risky; the old know that one of the greatest risks is to play it safe. For a life of too little risk has only one certainty: a future of regret.

Imagine yourself twenty years from today. What is running through your mind? Are you troubled by the risks you took that didn't work out? Or are you at peace with those decisions, knowing that at least you tried, and instead you regret the opportunities that you let roll right by?

Often, an opportunity presents itself but once. If you don't grab it in that moment, you've lost it. Another may come along someday, but that specific opportunity is gone. So keep in the forefront of your mind that if you don't take risks—or don't take *enough* risks—you guarantee yourself a future of regret.

There are many dangers in life. Safety is one of them.

> *Life is inherently risky. There is only one big risk you should avoid at all costs, and that is the risk of doing nothing.*
>
> **—Denis Waitley**

Doing nothing. Staying the same. Not growing, developing, or learning. Not pushing yourself. Those are some of the greatest risks you can take in life. Why? Because you end up living a life that is but a fraction of the one you could have lived.

It happens all the time: people live their entire lives in their comfort zone. Can you blame them? It's nice and warm, and there's a pleasing absence of any sort of awkward or unsettling emotions. It's like being inside a cozy house in wintertime. But it is also a farce, because there's a countdown timer. And the moment it strikes zero, a knock comes at the door. The fire goes out. Cold air rushes into the house. And in walks Regret.

The problem is not that the individual desires shelter and warmth. The problem is inherent in human psychology: We usually can see the possibility of a *near-term negative* outcome. But the possibility of a *long-term positive* outcome is a lot harder to spot. Short-term pain is clear; long-term gain is obscure.

As a result, we do our best to avoid short-term consequences (like the effort of reading a difficult book), but often at the expense of long-term benefits (like having a sound education).

Think a little harder for a little longer, and try to evaluate the short- *and* long-term implications of your decisions.

Exposing yourself to risk in the short term is the only way to reap reward in the long term. And the price for doing nothing—becoming stagnant—is one of the highest prices you can ever pay.

> *You can fail on what you don't want, so you might as well take a chance on doing what you love.*
>
> **—Jim Carrey**

No matter what you're doing, where you're doing it, or who you're doing it with, an element of risk is always there. But beware the biggest risk of all: spending a lifetime toiling away at something you don't love doing. You get only one shot at life; that's it. Wouldn't it be better to take a risk on doing what you love than to squander your limited time on something else?

Never be afraid to follow your dreams. Never apologize for doing what you feel is right in your heart. And never let the opinions of others compromise your own inner voice. For if you do, you may be taking the greatest risk you could ever take: spending your life living up to someone else's expectations.

Dealing with Fear and Risk Aversion

You can conquer almost any fear if you will only make up your mind to do so. For remember, fear doesn't exist anywhere except in the mind.

—Alfred A. Montapert

Success demands risk, and inherent in risk is fear. That's why, if we wish for success, we must learn to conquer our fears.

The problem is, fear is a powerful emotion. Fear can destroy dreams. Fear can squash hope. Fear can age us, paralyze us, and trample our dreams into the mire. What can we do to get the upper hand?

The first step is to see fear for all it really is: thought accompanied by feeling. The second step is to face it head-on—to tackle your fears daily and start building your reservoir of courage.

A useful technique here is to imagine the worst that can happen, assume that it occurs, and then work through what you would do in that situation. In doing this, we often reveal just how greatly we have exaggerated our fears.

Fear, like taxes, is inescapable. But while you may never escape your fears, you can learn to conquer them.

Fearlessness is like a muscle. I know from my own life that the more I exercise it the more natural it becomes to not let my fears run me . . . Being fearless has been the foundation of any success I have enjoyed—both personally and professionally.

—Arianna Huffington

How do we become better in business, sport, or any other part of life? We practice. The same is true for learning to control our fears.

Training begins by accurately identifying what you are afraid of. Next, make a verbal *and* written commitment to yourself to face your fears whenever they confront you—to feel the fear and take action anyway. And finally, honor that commitment.

What would your life look like if you didn't let your fears hold you back? On the other side of your fears, your wildest dreams await.

> *I learned that courage was not the absence of fear, but the triumph over it. The brave man is not he who does not feel afraid, but he who conquers that fear.*
>
> **—Nelson Mandela**

No matter who we are or how successful we are, we still have our fears. Indeed, it seems that fear is inseparable from the fabric of life. But to feel fear is not to be weak; it is to be human. So the question becomes, if we cannot free ourselves of our fears, what *can* we do? Here's what: we can make our fears work for us, not against us. The trick is to choose wisely what we fear.

For we can choose to fear mediocrity more than we fear failure. We can choose to fear complacency more than we fear discomfort. And we can choose to fear making no choice more than we fear making the wrong choice.

We all have our fears, but some fears are more useful than others. Choose yours wisely.

You can't connect the dots looking forward; you can only connect them looking backward. So you have to trust that the dots will somehow connect in your future. You have to trust in something: your gut, destiny, life, karma, whatever—because believing that the dots will connect down the road will give you the confidence to follow your heart, even when it leads you off the well-worn path, and that will make all the difference . . . Have the courage to follow your heart and intuition. They somehow already know what you truly want to become.

—Steve Jobs

It's easier to take greater risks when we have an unwavering faith that things will work themselves out in the end. But how do we develop such a mind-set? It usually happens in one of two ways.

Some people experience an inexplicable event that leads them to believe there is something out there bigger than all of us. And whatever it is, it's watching out for them. Others find a purpose that they are so passionate about, they're willing to do almost anything for it. To them, not chasing their dreams is the greatest risk they face.

If you don't happen to fit either of these descriptions, that's okay. You don't need faith to take a blind leap; you need only a good reason. Here it is: The only way to live your life to the fullest is to listen to the subtle voice of your innermost self, trust your intuition, and leap into uncertainty, in the direction you feel is right, believing that the dots will connect themselves down the road.

Flying into darkness can be scary. But it is nowhere near as frightening as living a life that doesn't follow your heart.

Reas'ning at every step he treads,

Man yet mistakes his way,

While meaner things, whom instinct leads,

Are rarely known to stray.

—William Cowper

Our subconscious is a master of observing, evaluating, and assessing the world, and then sending us signals based on what it finds. Yet we often ignore what it tells us, while—puzzlingly—we listen attentively to, and act promptly on, the opinions of others.

Part of the reason why we do this is because we are plagued by self-doubt. We don't truly believe that we are worthy of being great—or even of being above average. And why would we listen to someone who isn't even above average? Who are they to guide us toward success?

Developing a trust for what your intuition is telling you is one of life's great challenges. Those who do not trust themselves will never reach their full potential, and those who do will be empowered to create the life of their dreams.

Part of building this trust involves recognizing your self-worth: acknowledging the accomplishments you have achieved, reflecting on the skills you have acquired, being proud of the self-discipline you have developed, celebrating the philosophy you have cultivated, and relishing the potential of your future.

Once you comprehend that you *are* valuable, you give yourself permission to listen to your intuition and leap into the unknown, with faith that you can surmount whatever challenges come your way.

The irony of logic is that it tells us to listen to intuition.

And so . . .

Change, risk, and success are intricately interwoven—you can't have one without the others.

The process of changing ourselves and transforming our lives can be vexing, but only until we understand how the change process works.

The first thing to realize is that no one else can change you; only you can change you. And to do that, you must first observe yourself objectively so that you become aware of the need for change. Then, to create effective change, direct your energy toward changing what is on the inside—*before* you bother with what's on the outside.

Risk permeates the universe. It's unavoidable. So instead of trying to avoid risk, seek to take risks wisely. Here's how:

1. Understand your level of risk tolerance.

2. Seek the right *kinds* of risks (the kinds that will lead you away from regret and toward your dreams).

3. Do your best to minimize unnecessary risk.

4. Bear in mind the relationship between risk and reward.

5. Acknowledge that the greatest risk is *too little risk*, stagnation, and spending your life trying to meet someone else's expectations.

6. Leverage your courage, faith, and intuition to help overcome your fears and aversion to risk.

If you want to keep on getting what you're getting, keep on doing what you're doing. Otherwise, it's time to start embracing change and taking risks.

Work Well with Others and Strive Toward Leadership

Many People Make the Empire

Walk in Their Shoes

Conformity Is Not Harmony

Communicate Effectively

Enlightened Self-Interest: Help Others to Help Yourself

Leadership: It's a *Skill*

Leadership: It's about Others

~~~

NO ONE EVER achieved anything great acting alone, which is why, to accomplish our goals, we must learn to work well with others.

The trouble is, each of us has different ambitions in life, each of us is heavily influenced by the culture we grew up in, and each of us often struggles to articulate what we are thinking or feeling.

It is possible to deal with this complexity found in both human nature and human interaction. But to do so, we must deepen our understanding of human behavior and hone our communication skills.

We should also know that leadership is an option available to all of us. But only if we earn it. For leadership is not something we simply have or are given. It is a privilege that we make ourselves worthy of. And only after taking the time and effort required to develop the skills of leadership can we be entrusted with the opportunity to lead.

We are all in this together. Why not learn how to get along better? Why not learn how to lead yourself and others more effectively?

Many People Make the Empire

There are no problems which we cannot solve together, and there are very few which any of us can settle by himself.

—Lyndon B. Johnson

Each of us needs all of us to succeed. No one person can create a great nation, build a successful company, foster a loving family, or cultivate a supportive friendship. And no one person can solve any of the many challenging problems that exist today and that will exist in future.

It takes just a little experience in life to recognize how profoundly and quickly our ideas can improve when we discuss them with others. This is why the greatest achievements in history came out of groups of men and women working together in collaboration.

None of us is perfect, and neither are our ideas. But together, we can often get pretty darn close.

It marks a big step in your development when you come to realize that other people can help you do a better job than you could do alone.

—Andrew Carnegie

Let's be clear: it is *impossible* to achieve success without the help of others along the way, and this is truer today than ever before.

That's because we live in the most volatile, complex, and uncertain world that has ever been. And the only way to effectively navigate such a landscape is by assembling the strengths, perspectives, ideas, and creative flair of a *variety* of people and getting them all to give their best and work together in harmony.

Alone, we are weaker and life is smaller. Don't let your ego get in the way of working well with other people. You need them, and they need you.

We're an adaptable species. For all our failings, despite our limitations and fallibilities, we humans are capable of greatness.

—**Carl Sagan**

At some stage of our lives, each of us will succumb to selfishness or jealousy and will ruin relationships. Each of us will be tempted by shortcuts and perhaps jeopardize a project. And each of us will fall prey to the human tendency for self-deception and stubbornly refuse to change our ways.

While it's easy to dwell on the past and hold on to the many mistakes we have made—as siblings, parents, spouses, friends, and colleagues—this provides little benefit to our lives.

A wiser move is to forgive and move forward, for although we all make mistakes, we all still need each other. And we all still have the potential to rise above our failings. Our optimism can outshine our pessimism, our generosity can outweigh our greed, and our love can overpower our hate.

Don't be too quick to condemn, or too slow to forgive. We are all in this together.

Walk in Their Shoes

*Any fool can criticize, condemn and complain—and
most fools do. But it takes character and self-control to
be understanding and forgiving.*

—Dale Carnegie

Working effectively with others demands understanding and for-
giveness. This stems from empathy, the ability to walk in another's shoes and to know what they are feeling and experiencing.

Empathy takes practice. It is human nature to be absorbed
in ourselves, not in the cares and concerns of others. That's why
we must evolve the ways we think, feel, and respond. We must
train ourselves to tune in to other people's perspective, so we can
better understand what they are thinking and feeling and what
motivates them.

Be careful here. When it comes to your perceptions about you,
concern yourself less about what others think and more about
what *you* think (as we discussed in Pillar 1). But when it comes to
the thoughts and feelings of others, do the opposite. Place yourself in *their* world.

It's surprising how different the world can look when you're
standing in someone else's shoes.

*Each man calls barbarism whatever is not his own
practice; for indeed it seems we have no other test of
truth and reason than the example and pattern of the
opinions and customs of the country we live in.*

—Michel de Montaigne

Notions of what is normal and what is strange vary by place and
time. And it appears that our definition of "normality" captures
only a fraction of what is, in fact, reasonable.

Have you heard of the Phuket Vegetarian Festival in Thailand? Putting to shame the firewalking and blade-ladder climbing that are standard fare, men and women perforate their cheeks and tongues with knives, swords, and skewers, in bewildering acts of self-mutilation. It is believed that spirits or gods possess their bodies, so that the person feels no pain.

On the other side of the world, in the Amazon Basin, live the Yanomami people. Ritual practitioners of endocannibalism, they cremate and consume the bones of their deceased fellows. The practice is believed to strengthen the tribe and keep alive the spirit of the deceased.

And a few thousand miles north, in the United States, another peculiar tradition takes place: children who have lost a tooth put it underneath their pillow, to be collected by the Tooth Fairy. That's in exchange for some money, of course.

When working with others, try to remember that each of us is naturally biased by the culture we grew up in—its unspoken standards, expectations, and traditions. Keep an open mind, and don't be too quick to judge or dismiss, because people know only what they have been exposed to.

There is no such thing as normal; there is only culture. Don't fall prey to the ignorant belief that *the* world is the same as *your* world.

> *It is tempting, when we are hurt, to believe that the thing which hurt us intended to do so.*
>
> **—Alain de Botton**

At times, other people's actions are sure to leave us feeling annoyed, angered, or humiliated. But it's important to remind ourselves that many factors can influence what people say and do. And these often have little to do with us.

If you come home to find your spouse in a foul mood, it may be because of problems at work. If your boss seems especially irritable today, complications at home could be the cause. And if your parents can't help expressing their distaste with your life choices, perhaps it is because they grew up in a different time, place, or culture. Part of working effectively with others is being aware of this phenomenon and handling it gracefully, with empathy.

Not everything that happens to you happens because of you, nor does it necessarily reflect anything about you. Try to look at situations holistically. Try to see the complexity behind the action.

> *If I had asked people what they wanted, they would have said faster horses.*
>
> **—Henry Ford**

In business and in life, in dealing with customers, colleagues, friends, or family, most people have trouble articulating what they truly desire—because they don't really know what it is.

That's why, as you surely have witnessed many times, the thing people truly want or need is often different from what they tell you they want or need. And when they get what they asked for, they reject it.

This human tendency is unlikely to change anytime soon. But by becoming aware of it, we can protect ourselves from being led astray by well-intentioned but misleading words.

Pay close attention to what others are saying, but also observe their delivery. What do their facial expressions say? How about their body language? Tone of voice?

Words make up only a small part of a message. To receive the message in full, don't neglect the other parts.

Make the choice to care—decide the next person you talk to you are going to care. Look into their eyes; then get them to tell you a story—their story.

—Unknown

We are the intellectual species. And we are also deeply emotional beings. This is why the debate on whether reason rules emotion, or emotion rules reason, has been playing out for thousands of years.

The relationship between reason and emotion is complex. But we need only observe what goes on around us and within us to realize that we are driven primarily by emotion. We tend to act based on how we *feel*, not on what we think.

That's why it's important to reflect on the emotional impact you are having on others. Does your presence tend to stifle the room, or do people feel at ease around you? Does the way you communicate demonstrate that you care about others, or does it paint a portrait of selfishness?

People may forget what you said, and people may forget what you did, but they seldom forget how you made them feel.

Conformity Is Not Harmony

Madness is rare in individuals—but in groups, parties, nations, and ages it is the rule.

—Peter Thiel

Ever hear of Kitty Genovese? She was stabbed to death in New York City. Thirty-eight witnesses heard her cries for help, yet did nothing. Or perhaps you've heard about the infamous Jonestown, in northwestern Guyana? The place where more than 900 civilians committed suicide by ingesting cyanide, acting under the orders of their leader, Jim Jones.

These are extreme examples of an all-too-common phenomenon: people tend to do what other people are doing, and tend not to do what others are not doing—even if conforming doesn't make sense.

Working well with others doesn't mean simply agreeing with others or following the herd. Far from it. As the examples above demonstrate, taking your cue from those around you can lead to disaster. Just as importantly, the only way to arrive at the best possible outcome is to encourage, and then work through, disagreement.

The most successful families, organizations, communities, and nations succeed because people think for themselves and don't simply fall into step with group consensus.

Are you thinking for yourself?

In the challenge of building your ambition, stepping up to the opportunity and refining your thoughts and character, let everybody else lead small lives, but not you. Let everybody else cry over small hurts, but not you. Let everybody else argue over nonessentials, but not you. Deal in things that matter—the larger challenges, the larger opportunities.

—Jim Rohn

Many of us let ourselves slip into *smallness* in the way we think, dream, and act.

We give in to the temptation of gossip, bicker, and blame and let them sour our thoughts. We succumb to fear, complacency, or the norms of society and relinquish our dreams. And we sacrifice our integrity and our honor for small and ultimately insignificant gains.

But just because other people act in a certain way doesn't mean you have to. To be small, or not to be, is a choice available to each of us. What do you choose?

Is it so bad, then, to be misunderstood? Pythagoras was misunderstood, and Socrates, and Jesus, and Luther, and Copernicus, and Galileo, and Newton, and every pure and wise spirit that ever took flesh. To be great is to be misunderstood.

—Ralph Waldo Emerson

People yearn to be accepted, to feel part of a group and not to be different or misunderstood—it's human nature.

The first issue with this is that success won't ever come if we do not strive to live true to ourselves in thought, word, and action. That's why it is vital to protect your unique identity and not sacrifice who you are for the approval of others—even those closest to you.

This doesn't mean you shouldn't seek to improve who you are. Indeed, one of the most important pursuits in life is to maximize the best in us and minimize the worst. The point is that sacrificing our dreams for the chance of being accepted is a recipe for a midlife crisis or, worse still, an end-of-life crisis.

The second issue is that, by definition, the "greats" are distinct from the majority. If we want to join the ranks of the few, we must leave the ranks of the many. This isn't arrogance—we are no *better* than others. But we can be *different*. We can think differently, speak differently, and act differently. And if we are being self-disciplined and committed to our dreams, this will happen naturally.

Being different isn't easy. For it is, in essence, a deliberate alienation of yourself from the majority. Few people can do that, and few people achieve greatness.

Protect your unique self. And know that with greatness often comes estrangement.

The wise man is self-sufficient in that he can do without friends, not that he desires to do without them.

—Seneca

Success requires that we work with others to achieve our goals. And it also requires that we be self-reliant. Understandably, this can be confusing. But these seemingly opposing perspectives can be reconciled. The key lies in understanding the subtleties of self-reliance.

Self-reliance does not mean doing everything yourself. That would be close to impossible, and certainly a poor use of time. Rather, self-reliance means recognizing that even though you may not be responsible for doing the work, you are accountable for the result. The buck always stops with you.

So it must also be with our friends: Our friends contribute an important part to a successful life. But ultimately, we must be strong enough in our sense of self that if we happen to find ourselves alone, we are still in good company.

When you resist the urge to conform, tension will undoubtedly arise. Cultivate the strength to stand alone.

Communicate Effectively

The difference between the almost right word and the right word is really a large matter—'tis the difference between the lightning-bug and the lightning.

—Mark Twain

Effective communication is fundamental to teamwork, leadership, and success. But what is it and how do we learn it?

At its core, effective communication is the skillful use of language. It is the ability to affect others by delivering a compelling message in a compelling way—a message that is clear, persuasive, and tailored to the appropriate context and environment. It enables us to influence, motivate, and inspire others by painting a picture that guides them forward.

This isn't a talent we are born with. It's a skill that we must learn. We must practice our delivery; deepen our understanding of ourselves, others, and the world; build our vocabulary; speak with empathy; and learn to read our audience.

Devote the time to develop effective communication skills. It adds value in every arena of life.

When dealing with people, let us remember we are not dealing with creatures of logic. We are dealing with creatures of emotion, creatures bristling with prejudices and motivated by pride and vanity.

—Dale Carnegie

How people feel, not how they think, tends to define their behavior. That's why our emotional quotient—our "EQ"—is the foundation that effective communication skills are built on.

How's your EQ? Are you aware of the different emotions that arise and pass away within you? Are you aware of the emotions that you engender in other people? And do you recognize the triggers that bring about emotion, both in yourself and in others?

With a low EQ, we struggle to decipher how other people are feeling. That makes it difficult to deliver the right words in the right way, and also to assess how compelling our message was. Without those skills, we can't be effective communicators.

Work on your EQ. The effectiveness of your communication with friends, family, colleagues, and even utter strangers depends on it.

People always act on the basis of what they believe. If you want to change their actions (or your own), you have to change their beliefs.

—Michael Hyatt

Working well with others requires skill in the art of persuasion, influence, and motivation. What some people don't understand is that these skills are less about changing other people and more about helping others change themselves.

But even with that knowledge, the challenge still remains: how do you help others change what they believe? The trick is to target both the heart and the mind. Logic and argument have their place, certainly, but only after the right emotional buttons have been pushed.

Start talking to people's emotions. Get them to *feel* your message. Paint a picture or, better yet, immerse them by taking them into an environment that amplifies your message.

Experiences that don't touch the heart have only a small impact. The emotional level, like a boardroom, is where the big decisions are made.

Let your criticism enhance the life of the recipient. Let that person feel that you are interested in them, that you are willing to spend time and energy for them . . . It is easy to criticize; it is difficult to correct.

—Unknown

In life, we inevitably find ourselves in situations, both personal and professional, that rightly demand our criticism or even anger.

The problem is that we are emotional creatures at heart. So when we receive criticism or are confronted by anger, we tend to go on the defensive. And that makes for a delicate situation.

When delivering criticism, admonish the deed, not the doer. Criticize the action, not the person. And make sure the recipient of your criticism knows you *care*. When people feel that you care about them—about their growth and development—they are far less defensive.

With well-chosen and carefully delivered words, you can express criticism and anger in a constructive way. A valuable skill, to say the least.

Anyone can become angry—that is easy. But to be angry with the right person, to the right degree, at the right time, for the right purpose, and in the right way, that is not within everybody's power and is not easy.

—Aristotle

Effective communication requires that we speak the right words at the right time, with the right emotional tone. It hinges on our ability to rise above our current emotional state and make decisions based on what is best for us and others, not on how we feel in that moment.

Cultivating this skill begins with understanding that our feelings are the result of chemical reactions in our body. And with practice, it's possible to observe our emotions and let them run their course, instead of letting them consume and control us.

Next, we must understand that no one else can *make* us feel anything. The reality is that our mind interprets situations or events in a particular way, and then we translate that interpretation into an emotional response, positive or negative. If you find yourself entertaining an unproductive emotional state, consider how you have interpreted the situation at hand and whether or not that view is something you can change.

Anger can rise up suddenly, as can jealousy, disdain, and disgust. To be an effective communicator, you can't afford to let such impulses control you.

Enlightened Self-Interest: Help Others to Help Yourself

You can get everything in life you want, if you will just help enough people get what they want.

—Zig Ziglar

At the core of success is the concept of enlightened self-interest. This philosophy recognizes that helping others is your best path to success.

When you genuinely help others achieve their goals, you start developing a network that will give back far greater value than your initial investment. Contacts can be shared, introductions made, feedback received. And suddenly, you've got yourself a sound basis for support and growth.

The trouble is that we tend to be overly concerned with ourselves. We get so caught up in *our* desires, frustrations, and problems that we have no energy left to pay attention to others.

To work better with others, shift your focus and adjust your awareness. Whatever you're doing, ask yourself: How can I help this person, group, or situation? What can I do to add or create value here?

When you start thinking about others and how you can improve *their* lives, the world takes on a whole new look and feel.

It won't always be clear, but when you help someone else, you're helping yourself.

Giving, it turns out, is a very selfish act.

—Jay Samit

Life is often paradoxical. One of the most important paradoxes to understand is that the best way to receive and accumulate more is to give more. For when we *truly* give, which means giving with no expectation of anything in return, we usually receive back in far greater quantity.

Gifts don't have to be monetary. A genuine smile, a helping hand, a few kind words, all go a long way, especially in the hurried, full-steam-ahead culture so prevalent today.

Lend a little extra time, put in a little extra thought, devote a little extra care. *Give*, and you shall be repaid handsomely.

> *Thousands of candles can be lit from a single candle, and the life of the candle will not be shortened.*
>
> **—Federation of All Young Buddhist Associations of Japan**

The world can be divided into two groups of people: those who share and those who don't. Let's call them the sharers and the nonsharers.

The nonsharers are protective of their ideas, thoughts, and knowledge. Often, they fear being judged, or that others will "take" what they have. The sharers, on the other hand, pour out what they have, releasing value into the world for others to grab on to.

The problem with being a nonsharer is that judgment is unavoidable. More importantly, it's a great source for growth. And while others *might* take what you have, more often than not they don't steal your idea. Rather, they share it with others in a way that benefits you. And if they do try to steal it, they tend to fail at executing, because they don't have the passion to see it through.

Nonsharers also miss out on the benefits of being a sharer. Sharing with others—experiences you've had, books you've read, lessons you've learned, wisdom you've gained—reinforces these things within your own psyche. It also develops a mutual trust and respect that is critical to building relationships.

Share. It makes you stronger and the world a better place.

Leadership: It's a *Skill*

> *Leaders are made, they are not born. They are made by hard effort, which is the price which all of us must pay to achieve any goal that is worthwhile.*
>
> **—Vince Lombardi**

Leadership is difficult and demanding. But it is a skill that you can learn—if you take the time and put in the effort. Even the so-called natural-born leaders have weaknesses that they must find and deal with if they are to become exceptional leaders.

But leadership is not for everyone. As you ponder whether it is appealing to you, consider the following:

1. Leadership is one of the best ways to make a difference in other people's lives. It can be a source of great fulfillment.

2. Just as there are highs, there will be lows. Leadership can also be a source of great frustration and disappointment.

3. If you want to be a leader, you've got to earn it. Find the books. Seek out the mentors. Study, practice, and teach.

Becoming a leader rests on your desire to lead and on your willingness to earn that right.

> *The challenge of leadership is to be strong, but not rude; to be kind, but not weak; to be bold, but not a bully; to be thoughtful, but not lazy; to be humble, but not timid; to be proud, but not arrogant; to have humor, but without folly.*
>
> **—Jim Rohn**

Leadership is an ongoing, delicate balancing act between often opposing forces.

A leader is caring but unattached, encouraging but candid, and protecting but exposing.

A leader facilitates an environment of optimism, enthusiasm, and celebration but also has to make hard and often unpopular calls that can quickly sour the mood.

And a leader improves skills and builds self-confidence by constantly coaching the team, yet must also play the skeptic, scrutinizing information and decisions in a manner that some may see as bordering on mistrust.

You can learn this balance. But it comes only from a commitment to studying and practicing the art of leadership: developing and refining your leadership style and skill set in a never-ending cycle.

Leadership is like tightrope walking. The difference is, you're not alone on the tightrope.

The art of leadership is in the ability to make people want to work for you, while they are really under no obligation to do so.

—Haile Selassie

Asoka the Great, Napoleon Bonaparte, George Washington, Nelson Mandela, Martin Luther King Jr., and Mahatma Gandhi were *leaders*. The reason is that the people who followed them did so not because they had to, but because they wanted to.

Most aspiring leaders understand this much. What they often miss is that the best way to attract others to follow you is not by trying to convince them that they should. Rather, it is by trying to become someone worth following. That means working on your skills, working on your philosophy, working on everything you need to work on, so that you become someone people *want* to follow.

What you are, you attract. When you demonstrate dedication, the dedicated will come to you. When you demonstrate discipline, the disciplined will come to you. And when you demonstrate intelligence, the intelligent will come to you.

If you desire leadership, start working on yourself. Great leaders are always accompanied by voluntary followers.

> *Leaders conquer the context—the volatile, turbulent, ambiguous surroundings that sometimes seem to conspire against us and will surely suffocate us if we let them—while managers surrender to it.*
>
> **—Chérie Carter-Scott**

Leadership and management are very different modes of operation. Don't get them confused.

Management is about getting others to perform a set of tasks efficiently and effectively in order to achieve a specific, clearly defined goal. Leadership, on the other hand, is successfully navigating unknown terrain to reach an often unknown destination. It requires bringing together a group of people, creating a harmonious work environment, facilitating growth and development, and providing inspiration by means of a compelling vision.

Both management and leadership are important skills. Managers can be wonderfully useful in situations of stability. And leaders are essential when the circumstances are especially obscure or daunting. The issue is that many can manage, but few can lead. And that's a problem, because the world that awaits us grows more uncertain by the day.

We need great leaders. There's no reason you can't be one of them.

Leadership: It's about Others

Leadership is not magnetic personality—that can just as well be demagoguery. It is not "making friends and influencing people"—that is flattery. Leadership is lifting a person's vision to higher sights, the raising of a person's performance to a higher standard, the building of a personality beyond its normal limitations.

—Peter F. Drucker

Leadership is about other people. It is about identifying their dreams and desires and enabling their growth and success. But there are two distinct parts to facilitating positive change in other people's lives. And most of the time, we remember only one of them.

The part we tend to forget, which happens to be the more difficult part, is the exposing of errors. Here, a leader transports others into their past, showing them clearly the mistakes they have made and making them aware of the need for change.

The other part (and this part is more fun) is painting a picture of the possibilities. This means transporting others into the future to show them the person that they could become, and the life they could live, thus helping them ignite the fire of their motivation.

When it stops being about what you want and starts being about others, you're on the right path to leadership.

All of the great leaders have had one characteristic in common: it was the willingness to confront unequivocally the major anxiety of their people in their time. This, and not much else, is the essence of leadership.

—John K. Galbraith

The implicit promise of leadership is this: I will solve a problem for you. Follow me, and your life will improve.

Naturally, the problems will vary in type and magnitude. And many times, people may not even know they have a problem that needs solving. Still, anyone seeking a leadership role must ask: Why should anyone follow me? What's in it for them? What problem am I helping them solve? How am I contributing to their better life?

If you want people to follow you, give them a good reason why they should. Help them solve their problems.

> *If your actions create a legacy that inspires others to dream more, learn more, do more and become more, then you are an excellent leader.*
>
> **—Dolly Parton**

The ability to inspire others to stand taller, reach higher, dream bigger, and step out of their comfort zones is perhaps the most valuable leadership skill.

The trouble is that each of us differs in our dreams, desires, and passions, and also in our frustrations, fears, and foibles. With around 100 billion neurons in the brain, connected by trillions of synapses, suffice it to say that we humans are complex beings.

Because of this complexity, the ability to inspire others demands a certain degree of mental and emotional maturity. And that takes time to develop. The good news is that to start working on it, you don't need others. You already have the perfect test case: yourself.

Become your own leader. It may sound odd, but on closer inspection of our lives, we realize that we are often unable to guide and motivate ourselves effectively toward success. Granted, sometimes it's easier to guide others than to guide ourselves. But this just makes our lives an even better training ground.

Leadership *is* about others. But before you start trying to lead others, try to see whether you can lead yourself.

And so . . .

You can't achieve your goals by yourself, which is why the ability to work well with others is such a critical part of success.

Developing this skill begins with deepening your understanding of human behavior: becoming aware that culture dramatically affects lives; understanding that many factors influence actions; remembering to read between the lines of what people are saying; and recognizing that conformity leads to neither harmony nor progress.

The last point is an important one. Herd mentality, the tendency to do something because others are doing it, is real—and frightening. It challenges independent thought, which has been the foundation for all major human advancement. Each of us must resist the urge and overcome the challenge, for blindly following others benefits no one.

Next, strive to become an effective communicator. This means learning to connect with others on the emotional level, targeting both the heart and the mind with your messages. And it requires being aware of when your emotions start controlling you.

These steps also happen to be steps toward leadership. For as we deepen our understanding of ourselves and others and we learn how to deliver messages that educate, motivate, and inspire, we begin developing a mental and emotional maturity that is a core part of the leadership skill set.

Working well with others is crucial to success. And it is through leadership that you may find some of life's greatest treasures. But these are skills that you must learn before you can reap the benefits.

See the Big Picture

The Nature of Life

Meet the Teacher; Her Name Is Death

There We Are. That Little Speck. See It?

Check the Price Tag

More than Meets the Eye

WHEN YOU ARE running a race, the crowd disappears, and your daily worries slip to the back of your mind. You are focused solely on what you have to do right now: place one foot in front of the other, and repeat. Anything beyond that 400-meter cinder loop isn't even in your frame of reference.

This can also be a metaphor for our lives. We can get so caught up in everyday events, at home and at work, that before we realize it, a decade has sailed right past us. That's why we must remember, every now and then, to step back and see the big picture.

Here we all are, thrown together on planet Earth. It can feel downright chaotic sometimes. There's good weather and bad, with mountains to climb and rivers to cross. And our lives are a little like a house of cards outside in the open: fragile and temporary.

Yes, *temporary*. Whether we like it or not, death is an inescapable reality of life. And every one of us should keep this awareness. Why? Because to ignore death is to ignore a great and wise teacher.

Just as important as the awareness of death is the awareness of our place in the universe. It's a tiny, minuscule dot in a vast galaxy among billions of other vast galaxies, but it's the only place we have. On this planet, we will live out our lives and leave our legacy. And as we walk this path, we should keep an eye on the tab, because not everything is worth the price.

Success demands focus. But don't forget about the big picture.

The Nature of Life

After climbing a great hill, one only finds that there are many more hills to climb.

—Nelson Mandela

Growth, success, and life are cyclical. That's why, when we make it to the top of one mountain, we are apt to discover another, higher peak before us.

What's interesting is that the specific mountain doesn't really matter. For whatever the mountain, the journey is similar. On every journey we are certain to meet with Struggle, Triumph, and Defeat.

When you meet with Struggle, embrace her. She is the seed of growth and transformation and will lead you toward Triumph.

When you meet with Triumph, give her a smile. Your time with Triumph is a well-deserved reward for your time with Struggle.

And when you inevitably meet with Defeat, meet her with humility—and with a short stay in mind. Dwell with her too long, and you may forget what Triumph looks like.

We all will experience the highs and the lows, the joys and the sorrows, the warm summers and bone-chilling winters. Embrace the cyclical nature of all that is.

There are fewer stories than there are people on earth, the plots repeated ceaselessly while the names and backdrops alter.

—Alain de Botton

The greatest works of art are those that speak to us without knowing of us, simultaneously capturing the uniqueness of an individual and the whole of human existence. Though the artists never knew us, we see ourselves in their work and understand ourselves better because of it.

How can this be? How can the great artists speak to us both individually and collectively at the same time? The reason is that we don't suffer alone, isolated and confused. Rather, we suffer together with all humankind.

All your heartbreak, stress, and fatigue; all your struggle, turmoil, and confusion; all your pain, regret, and indecision—all the trials that you experience in life—are also the experience of others.

We are all, literally, in this together.

> *The sun that shines today is the sun that shone when thy father was born, and will still be shining when thy last grandchild shall pass into the darkness.*
>
> **—George S. Clason**

The world today looks very different from a century ago. Gone are the whalebone corset, the black-and-white still photo, and the stock ticker, replaced by Victoria's Secret, the smartphone, and the Internet.

But although we dress differently, live more complicated lives, and communicate in completely different ways from our great-grandparents, life, at its core, is the same as it has always been.

Life continues to bring rain and sunshine. Tragedy and triumph come to us all. And sorrow and joy surround us by turns. Indeed, all the ingredients of life are to be found in each of our lives, no matter the time or place. And what we do with those ingredients is what makes the difference.

Life has always been and will forever be a mix of challenge and opportunity. What you make of it is up to you.

Truth does not need to be advertised.

—Unknown

Whether you acknowledge the truths of the universe is irrelevant, for the truth will go on existing just fine, with or without you.

One such truth is that the world is indifferent to you. For the world operates according to laws. There are laws of chemistry, mathematics, motion, gravity, thermodynamics, and so on. And as a by-product of these laws, every so often you will be presented with challenge. And every so often you will be presented with opportunity. Whether or not you rise to meet these challenges, or choose to grab the opportunities with both your hands, the world is unconcerned.

This is no reason to be disheartened. For this truth is a reminder that your life is completely up to you. There is no life you ought to lead, job you ought to get, or house you ought to buy. There is no degree you must earn. There are no risks you must take. And there is no one but yourself to please, impress, or convince that you are good enough.

But in the end, you *do* have to live with yourself. And that's far easier knowing that you gave your all and lived life to its fullest.

The world may not care about how you choose to live your life, but you can.

We must reconcile ourselves to the necessary imperfectibility of existence.

—Alain de Botton

Life is imperfect. There are wicked people who do wicked deeds. We have enemies who seek to do us harm. And even when we do everything right and justly deserve success, it doesn't always come to us. It's important to understand this.

It's also important to understand that many things in life are out of our control. And when we stop trying to control what we cannot control, or trying to change what we cannot change, we free up an enormous trove of time and energy for more productive uses.

Sometimes, the hailstorm destroys the crop. That's life. The question is: will we plant once more?

Meet the Teacher; Her Name Is Death

There may be no single thing that can teach us more about life than death.

—Arianna Huffington

Just as failure is a great teacher for success, so is death a great teacher for life.

Death will teach you that your time is limited, and that the gift of life comes with no guarantees on how long it will last.

Death will teach you that nothing is permanent: all structures inevitably crumble, and all things fade away into obscurity.

And death will teach you that love transcends far beyond the physical boundaries of this world—it is at once singular and obvious, infinite and fathomless.

Bring awareness to death and learn what it means to be alive. Memento mori.

A man who dares to waste one hour of time has not discovered the value of life.

—Charles Darwin

Every second that passes is lost to the universe. Every hour that goes is gone. And the dimming of the night sky marks that day's permanent and irrevocable end.

What is life but the use of time? What is life but the filling up of each second and hour with experiences that we take with us into the future?

Time is not to be feared, but it merits our respect. And by respecting time, we respect ourselves and our lives. The unfortunate reality is that we typically recognize a thing's value only *after* we have lost it. It's unfortunate because once we are out of time, that's it.

How many more years do you have left?

Death smiles at us all. All a man can do is smile back.

—Maximus Decimus Meridius (in *Gladiator*)

How close are we to the precipice of death? None of us knows. All we know is that the future is uncertain. We may live to be 100 or die at 25. Tomorrow could be our last day on this earth, or perhaps it is today. This may sound melodramatic, but that doesn't make it any less true.

What does this uncertainty—this fragility of life—mean for our lives? It's a good question to ask, isn't it? If the end were to come far sooner than you expected, what dreams would die with you? What adventures would you never have? What words would you leave unsaid? Could you say that you did all you could, gave all you had, and lived the best life possible?

Death is always waiting in the wings. Don't fear this; embrace it. Let death guide you toward a life of passion, focus, and intent. Let death enable you to spend your time and energy wisely so that when the end comes, you will pass with contentment.

Live with the knowledge that death is our constant companion; still fearsome, but an ally and source of wise counsel: constant awareness of the limit of our time and love.

—M. Scott Peck

The relationships we share with family, friends, and even strangers are among the most valuable gifts of life. Most of us are aware of this. What we tend to forget—or perhaps choose to ignore—is that these relationships are also temporary.

One day, we can be certain, they will cease. That loving smile we are so fond of, gone. That affectionate embrace that kept us warm at night, only a memory.

This should sadden you. It's important to grieve the loss of what had been a great joy. But don't let it *only* sadden you. Use this knowledge to bring into your life true appreciation and even greater love for those around you. Let the awareness of death help you cherish your relationships.

There is a limit to both your time and your love.

> *All things fade away, become the stuff of legend, and are soon buried in oblivion. Mind you, this is true only for those who blazed once like bright stars in the firmament, but for the rest, as soon as a few clods of earth cover their corpses, they are "out of sight, out of mind." In the end, what would you gain from everlasting remembrance? Absolutely nothing. So what is left worth living for? This alone: justice in thought, goodness in action, speech that cannot deceive, and a disposition glad of whatever comes.*
>
> **—Marcus Aurelius**

There will come a time when the lights go off. We know this in our heart of hearts, but this truth struggles to find its way into our daily lives. That's why we often are led astray by bright and shiny things that, in the end, hold little importance.

To be clear, success *is* about developing to your full potential and living life to the hilt. That could mean accomplishing your childhood dream of having your very own helicopter. Or, like Richard Branson, becoming a proud owner of an island. But as you go about turning your dreams into reality, be aware that all things eventually disappear into the ether.

That's why success is not about what we get; it is about what we become: a man or woman of virtue and reason, patience and kindness, wisdom and generosity.

Don't let this slip from your focus for too long. You are not promised this day or even this hour. Disaster can strike at any moment, and only those with their self-respect intact will leave this world in true peace and contentment.

Let death remind you what really matters.

> *Carve your name on hearts, not tombstones. A legacy is etched into the minds of others and the stories they share about you.*
>
> **—Shannon L. Alder**

When we are alive and kicking, it is easy to see the impact of our actions. We can see the knowledge we impart through mentoring others. We can feel the joy we bring with our gifts to family and friends. And the charities we support keep us updated on how they are using our donations.

But the impact we have on others and the world does not necessarily cease when we cease. It can continue through the legacy that we leave. And that legacy is being shaped by the decisions we make and the actions we take every day of our lives.

This can lead some people off course. They want so badly to make a contribution that they end up trampling over anyone in their way. So as you ponder the legacy you would like to leave, consider this:

It's not whether you won or lost that matters, only that you fought. It's not the words and judgments of those you didn't know that count; it's the respect of those you knew. If, at the end of your life, you have gained the admiration of your inner circle of family and friends—those who knew you best, who knew all your dreams, desires, commitment, and hard work—then you have lived well. And your legacy will reflect that.

How will you be remembered?

Being the richest man in the cemetery doesn't matter to me. Going to bed at night saying we've done something wonderful—that's what matters to me.

—**Steve Jobs**

If you live to be 85, you have around 31,000 days to use. By age 20, you would have some 24,000 days left. When you turn 40, 16,000 days would remain. And at age 60, you would have only 9,000 days left, or 300 months—and last month went by pretty quickly, didn't it?

Your time is finite. So what kind of life do you *want* to live? What sort of contribution do you want to make to the world? How do you want to spend your remaining days?

You are never too old (or too young) to set goals, chase dreams, or completely reinvent yourself. Let the awareness of death inspire you to come alive.

There We Are. That Little Speck. See It?

In the visible world, the Milky Way is a tiny fragment; within this fragment, the solar system is an infinitesimal speck, and of this speck our planet is a microscopic dot.

—Bertrand Russell

We are a tiny speck in a seemingly infinite universe. It's almost incomprehensible: there are more stars in the universe than there are grains of sand on earth. We are a blip in the night sky.

Herein lies a lesson in humility: In the grand scheme of things, we are inconsequential. But at the same time, we cannot help wondering: Are we not all there is, all we know, all that matters?

Against the backdrop of billions of years in an unfathomably vast, ever-expanding universe, our actions within the brief flicker of a single earthbound existence mean nothing. But here on earth, in daily life, we *can* make a significant impact on our lives, the lives of others, and the world we live in.

Don't forget that your actions are important, your life is meaningful, and you can make an impact. It took around 14 billion years for us to get here. Let's make the most of it.

Enlightenment and success are worth our sincerest efforts, but that doesn't mean we have to be so damn serious all the time. Seriousness is a terrible dis-ease. You catch it from striving too hard.

—Michael J. Carr

Ponder, for a moment, your intergalactic address: the tiny space you occupy in the street, suburb, city, country, continent, planet, and galaxy you call home. Does that not help put into perspective whatever dramas you have going in your life?

We all are temporary guests on this planet, and sometimes we should take things a little less seriously. The fate of civilization does *not* hinge on the annual board presentation. Things could be *much* worse than getting stuck in a traffic jam. And yes, the fight you had with your best friend is unfortunate, but it *doesn't* mean the world is ending.

Life is precious, and we should respect it by making the most of our limited time. But that doesn't mean *always* being serious.

> *We are born within a charmed circle of protection, never knowing its value till we wander into the disordered or solitary regions of the earth . . . We partake in a luxurious patrimony of social order built up for us by a hundred generations of trial and error, accumulated knowledge, and transmitted wealth.*
>
> **—Will Durant**

All around the world, progress has come in fits and starts. We are becoming more educated, living longer lives, and putting an end to all manner of needless pain, disease, and suffering.

To be sure, much work remains. But each of us should appreciate the benefits of the world we inhabit today—benefits we scarcely dreamed of even a few decades ago.

This is especially pertinent for those of us lucky enough to live in a safe and free country, with the rule of law, modern medicine, education, and democracy. We are protected by laws we didn't write. We can appeal to courts we didn't create, be healed with medicines we didn't develop, and learn from educational institutions we didn't found. And yet, we often take these incalculable blessings for granted.

Don't forget how lucky you are simply to be alive in this modern era.

We have not inherited this earth from our parents to do with it what we will. We have borrowed it from our children and we must be careful to use it in their interests as well as our own.

—Moses Henry Cass

The earth as we know it, and our place in it, has changed so dramatically since humans began, we can hardly imagine how it must have been: Without fire, darkness must have cowed us. Without social order, barbarism would have prevailed. And without science, we would have been living in ignorance.

We have come far as a species. But we can become so focused on advancement that we forget to think about the costs of our actions—especially to those who do not yet inhabit this planet.

The impact we are having on the earth is the subject of fierce debate. Regardless of our views on specific issues such as climate change, a philosophy of success insists that we leave everything in better condition than we found it. This includes the earth.

Protect and care for our beautiful planet. Let others enjoy its vibrant diversity of life just as we have.

Check the Price Tag

Man sacrifices his health to make money. Then he sacrifices his money to recuperate his health. And then he is so anxious about the future that he doesn't enjoy the present. As a result, he lives neither in the present nor in the future. He lives as if he were never going to die, and then dies never having really lived.

—Unknown

Everything in life has a price, and sometimes what we get is simply not worth what we paid.

What's the point of having a beach house in Malibu if you've got no friends or family to share it with? Where is the logic in having your own yacht if you don't have enough time to take it out on the open ocean? And what benefit is a large bank account when poor health cuts your life short by twenty years?

Before you begin chasing your dreams, try to gauge just how much it's going to cost you. What might be the price in health? What might be the toll on your relationships? What damage might it mean to your self-respect?

Life is not simply checking off goals and accumulating toys. Life is about finding what is truly important to you and then protecting that as if everything depended on it.

Determine carefully what you want to strive for, or you might lose something even greater in the striving.

When there's no one left to knife, and there's nothing you stand for, won't the knives be pointed at you?

—Nikos Mourkogiannis

Life is full of trade-offs, and the decisions we must make can be difficult, both for us and for those closest to us. There's no getting around it.

On the one hand, you should do what feels right in your heart. But you also need to be looking down the road at where your decisions are taking you. If, after all your hard work, struggle, and sacrifice, the life you end up with is not worth living, then all your efforts have gone for naught.

There is always a price to pay for success. Be mindful of who you are becoming and how you are acting in pursuit of your goals. Make sure you can afford the bill when it comes time to leave the table.

> *The great thing in the world is not so much to seek happiness as to earn peace and self-respect.*
>
> **—Thomas Huxley**

Each of us entered this world naked: free of possessions. We also entered this world innocent and uncorrupted. Fast-forward some eighty-odd years, and we leave this world naked once again. But innocent?

The sad reality is that during our lives, many of us will fail to serve the highest of all duties: to live a life worthy of our own self-respect. Many of us will turn our backs on the truth. Many of us will forgo our dreams. And many of us will sacrifice our integrity.

What we must realize is that our self-respect is perhaps the most precious thing there is. Self-respect cannot be bought or even sought. No one can give it to you. It is yours alone to nurture and protect; and it is yours alone to lose.

Never compromise your self-respect. Nothing is worth that price.

More than Meets the Eye

What lies behind us and what lies before us are tiny matters compared to what lies within us.

—Henry S. Haskins

Life is chaotic, but it can also be—even at the same time—serene and peaceful. This is because we have both an inner and an outer world. And while chaos may reign supreme out there, you have the power to create and sustain peace within. But that can come only if you make time to explore yourself.

Every day, close out the rest of the world, just for a little while. Give yourself the opportunity to ponder, wonder, pray; the opportunity to look within and to center yourself.

When you become centered, you walk through the world with peace and power emanating from deep within, regardless of what is happening on the outside.

Mastering your inner world requires a deep knowledge of your inner workings. And like all great journeys, it begins with a single step. Look inside.

Happiness is not an end—it is only a means, an adjunct, a consequence.

—Dinah M. Craik

We often think that our lives could be so much better and we could be so much happier if only we could get that promotion, buy that house, or go on that holiday. We are so busy waiting for the right set of circumstances to *finally* be happy, we don't realize that the only thing stopping us from being happy right now is *us*.

Happiness comes from within. You can't get it (not with any permanence, at least) from anything outside you. This becomes clear to the self-aware traveler who finds, whether in New York, Rome, Buenos Aires, or Moscow, that it's our same old self we see in the mirror.

You are the gatekeeper to your happiness. To be happy or not is your decision. And all that you need to be happy, you already have.

Men go forth to marvel at the heights of mountains and the huge waves of the sea, the broad flow of the rivers, the vastness of the ocean, the orbits of the stars, and yet they neglect to marvel at themselves.

—Saint Augustine

Self-appreciation is fundamental to living a successful life, and it has two distinct parts. Most people are aware of the first; fewer pay much attention to the second.

The first part of self-appreciation involves recognizing and celebrating just how far we've come on our journey. We reflect on the obstacles we have overcome, the skills we have developed, and the philosophy we have cultivated. Then we smile proudly.

The second part of self-appreciation is quite different. It involves stripping away all that we have and own, and appreciating ourselves for the marvelous human beings that we are, just as we are: so complex in biology and chemistry, so distinct in physical traits and in thought, so nuanced in behavior and emotion.

Acknowledge your accomplishments, but don't forget what a wondrous being you are even after setting aside the things you've done.

And so . . .

Life is a mix of challenge and opportunity. It has always been that way, and it will always be that way. The sun will continue to shine. Rain will continue to pour. And the winds of life will continue to blow. The question is, what will we make with the ingredients that life has given us?

The clock is forever counting down, and the time we have left to us is unknown. This can be so confronting that we don't talk about it. And that is a tragedy, because death can teach us so much about life.

Death can teach us to respect the limited time we have on this planet. (This creates a sense of urgency that is invaluable when chasing dreams.) Death can help us cherish our relationships with friends and family. Death can remind us to focus less on what we get, and more on what we become. And death can encourage us to leave a legacy that we are proud of.

We must become aware, not only of death, but also of our place in the universe. We inhabit a tiny speck of dust in a huge galaxy amid a seeming infinity of other galaxies. But that doesn't make our lives irrelevant. The actions we take every day have tangible effects on our lives and the lives of others. We mustn't forget that.

We also mustn't forget that everything in life comes at a price. The pursuit of our dreams can be a glorious undertaking, but only if we can hold on to our self-respect.

There is always a bigger picture. Step back and take a look.

Before You Go

Creating and living your best life is not easy, but it is simple. Let's reflect:

The Foundation: The first step toward success is to accept full responsibility for your life. This is your life and no one else's. You are the one living it. You are the one bearing the consequences of your actions. And it is up to you to take it in the direction you want it to go.

Pillar 1: It is your thoughts and your perceptions of yourself, others, and the world that truly define the life you live. In most cases, you are affected more by the way you *think* things are than by the way they actually are. That's why it is crucial to perceive the world to your advantage, not to your detriment.

Pillar 2: Complacency is one of life's greatest challenges. It's just too easy to find a place where we are comfortable . . . and then stop. But success means creating and living the *best* life possible for us, which means consciously avoiding this plateau by always striving for growth.

Pillar 3: Life is filled with distractions, and it can be tricky sorting out what's important and what isn't. You've got to identify what truly matters to you, and keep yourself focused and moving toward your dreams. So set your goals. Then plan and execute.

Pillar 4: There are just as many mirages of success as there are misunderstandings about failure. The ultimate success is being able to leave this life with contentment when death eventually comes. And it is through failing that we earn the right to succeed.

Pillar 5: No one else can change you. Only you can change you. And forget trying to avoid risk; it's impossible. Instead, strive to take the kinds of risks that move you toward your goals.

Pillar 6: You can't achieve success by yourself, which is why learning to work well with other people is crucial. This skill also opens the door to leadership. And through leadership, you may find some of life's greatest treasures.

Pillar 7: On your journey, don't become so obsessed with the task before you that you forget to step back and see the big picture. Life is fragile, unpredictable, and brief. And all the drama that comes with human existence is happening on a small planet in an obscure corner of an incomprehensibly vast universe. Still, it's all you have. Don't forget the miracle that is life.

You have now been exposed to wisdom from a wide sampling of history's greatest exemplars, encompassing all the fundamentals of success. Take this wisdom, ponder it, dissect it, debate it, refine it, share it, and apply it to your life.

And if you integrate only one thing from this book, let it be this: Find out how you want to spend your limited time on this planet. Find out what motivates you, energizes you, inspires you, and fulfills you. And once you know this, make it your focus. Defend your dreams against any erosive influence, be it friends, family, or society. Stand resolute on what is important to you. And strive every day toward creating and living the life you desire.

To your knowledge, understanding, and wisdom.

To your health, wealth, and happiness.

To your dreams.

To your achievement.

To the treasures of your heart, soul, and mind.

I leave you now, but the ideas from this book will remain.

Your friend,
James Melouney

If the insights shared in this book have inspired you, I would love to hear from you. You can reach me on social media or by e-mail. Better yet, stop by the website.

And if you have found this book useful, why don't you help a friend by passing it along? My only request is that you please leave an honest review on your platform of choice. Reviews are hard to come by, and I would greatly and sincerely appreciate the time investment that it requires from you.

@jmelouney
james@jamesmelouney.com
www.jamesmelouney.com

P.S. Don't forget to read Appendix 1: A Discussion on Success.

Appendix I

A Discussion on Success

By definition, success is the accomplishment of something that one has set out to accomplish. Following this, one may be successful in getting a particular job or achieving some other specific goal.

Over time, "success" evolved into something broader. It became synonymous with acquiring material possessions or becoming someone prominent in society.

The first flaw with this definition is that it's societal; it reflects a certain place and time and culture—in this instance, a capitalistic society in the Western world. The problem with societally based definitions is that they tend to be ill-suited to other societies. The mind-set, culture, and lifestyle of a typical United States citizen is almost irreconcilable with that of the Yanomami people of the Amazon Basin that we discussed earlier. Thus, a definition of success based on either society alone will likely hold little meaning for the other society.

The second flaw is a by-product of this particular definition of success being rooted in Western civilization: it is based on material possessions and prominence. And becoming a wealthy or prominent member of society is not the same as becoming a fulfilled member of society—or being successful.

Consider the tragic end to the lives of Robin Williams, Philip Seymour Hoffman, L'Wren Scott, and Ernest Hemingway. These men and women accomplished extraordinary things, but to end their lives in such a way indicates that their fame and fortune could not compensate for their sadness.

Our definition of success must grow broader still. It must take into account the world's great cultural and individual diversity. If the desires of the heart and mind happen to lead an individual down a road less traveled, that road is theirs to walk, and the measure of their success, or lack thereof, is theirs to decide.

And so we come to another definition of success: being able to leave this life with contentment when death eventually comes. This is the ultimate success in life. For it signifies that someone did all they could, gave all they had, and made the most of their time. It means that someone created the best life possible for *them*. What more can we do?

Underpinning this definition are four qualities that characterize success: success is relative, forward looking, twofold, and stretching. By understanding these elements, any of us can bring success within our reach.

Success is *relative*. It depends in part on the circumstances of your birth and life, and also on what you want to do while you are here. You cannot control where or when you are born, or to whom. All you can do is make the best of whatever start in life you had. And there is no prescribed path you must walk. You don't have to become a doctor, an entrepreneur, or a politician. You don't need to own a dozen properties and have a bulging bank account. You have a certain number of days to use, and you can use them however you desire. This is not to suggest that success comes of stumbling through life. Rather, it comes of identifying the kind of life that holds meaning for you, and then creating that life.

Success is *forward looking*. It encompasses both what you value now and what you will value in the future. For example, let's suppose you don't exercise regularly and you don't eat a nutritionally sound diet. In other words, at this current stage of your life, you don't particularly value your health. Experience suggests—anecdotally but emphatically—that as you grow older and more aware of the importance of health, you *will* value it. Thus, success for you includes good health, even though you don't value it right now. (This is why the successful life is ultimately a balanced life.)

Success is *twofold*. It is both an ongoing process and a final state. The former relates to *living successfully*, the latter to *being successful*. The degree to which you are successful depends on how close you are to achieving all that you ever desired to achieve. Those who are extraordinarily successful are on the cusp of accomplishing everything they set out to accomplish. Those who are moderately successful are, say, 25 to 75 percent of the way there. Whether you are *living successfully* depends on the actions you are taking in the present moment, and the extent to which those actions move you toward your best life. When you are giving all you have and doing your utmost to create the life you desire, then you are living successfully at that moment. Naturally, there are different degrees of living successfully, just as there are to being successful. And it almost goes without saying, the more time you spend living successfully, the more successful you're likely to be.

Finally, success is *stretching*. It takes into account how well you make use of the gifts you have been blessed with. Even if you truly desire to spend your life sitting around, and then you do that, you won't be counted among the ranks of the successful. Why? Because you could have done so much more but instead chose to squander your talents. And you will know this in your heart.

To summarize, success is . . .

1. *Relative.* It depends on your circumstances and your desires.

2. *Forward looking.* It includes what you value now and what you will value in the future.

3. *Twofold.* It is a final state that results from an ongoing process.

4. *Stretching.* It considers how well you make use of all your capacities.

Each of us can achieve success. The critical question is, how shall you live so that when death eventually comes, you leave this world with contentment?

APPENDIX 2

The Exemplars

All 134 exemplars are listed below, in alphabetical order, with a brief description. Credit goes to *Wikipedia* for much of the information.

Addison, Joseph, 1672-1719. English essayist, poet, playwright, and politician. Addison was a cofounder of *The Spectator* magazine and a member of the Irish House of Commons.

Alder, Shannon L, -. Author. Alder is known for her book *300 Questions to Ask Your Parents Before It's Too Late.*

Allen, James, 1864-1912. British philosophical writer. Allen is known for his inspirational books and poetry and as a pioneer in the self-help movement. His most prominent book is *As a Man Thinketh.*

Aristotle, 384-322 BC. Greek philosopher and scientist. Aristotle was a teacher of Alexander the Great, and a student of Plato. He was a prolific poet and writer on physics, biology, logic, ethics, and politics.

Atkinson, Brooks, 1894-1984. US theater critic. The *New York Times* called him "the theater's most influential reviewer of his time." New York's Brooks Atkinson Theater is named in his honor.

Aurelius, Marcus, 121-80. Roman emperor during 161-80. A stoic philosopher and author of the Stoic tome *Meditations*, he is regarded as the last of the "Five Good Emperors."

Bach, Richard, 1936-. US author of *Jonathan Livingston Seagull* and *Illusions: The Adventures of a Reluctant Messiah*. Most of his books are semiautobiographical, using actual and fictionalized events from his life to illustrate his philosophy.

Bacon, Francis, 1561-1626. English philosopher, statesman, scientist, jurist, and author. Bacon served as attorney general and lord chancellor of England. He is regarded by some as the "father of empiricism."

Baruch, Bernard M., 1870-1965. US financier, philanthropist, statesman, and political consultant. Baruch was economic adviser to Presidents Woodrow Wilson and Franklin Roosevelt.

Branson, Richard, 1950-. English businessman, investor, and philanthropist. Branson is known as cofounder (along with Nik Powell) of Virgin Group, which encompasses over 400 companies worldwide.

Brown, H. Jackson Jr., 1940-. US author. Brown is known for *Life's Little Instruction Book*, which he wrote as a going-away present for his college-bound son Adam.

Buffett, Warren, 1930-. US businessman, investor, and philanthropist. Perhaps the most successful investor ever, Buffet is the Chairman and CEO of Berkshire Hathaway. Buffet has signed the Giving Pledge, meaning he plans to give most of his net worth to philanthropic causes during his life or upon his death.

Burke, Edmund, 1729-97. Irish statesman, author, orator, political theorist, and philosopher. Burke is regarded by some as the "father of modern British conservatism."

Buscaglia, Leo, 1924-98. US author and motivational speaker, known as "Dr. Love." Five of Buscaglia's books were simultaneous *New York Times* best sellers.

Byron, George Gordon, 1788-1824. Commonly known as Lord Byron and regarded as one of the greatest British poets, he was a leading figure in the Romantic movement. He is known for his poems *Don Juan* and *Childe Harold's Pilgrimage*.

Carlyle, Thomas, 1795-1881. Scottish philosopher, satirist, essayist, historian, and mathematician. He is known for his book *The French Revolution: A History*.

Carnegie, Andrew, 1835-1919. Scottish-American industrialist and philanthropist. Carnegie drove the expansion of the American steel industry in the late nineteenth century. His philanthropic efforts included the donation of some 3,000 public libraries throughout the United States, Britain, Canada, and other English-speaking countries.

Carnegie, Dale, 1888-1955. US author, lecturer, and instructor in self-improvement, salesmanship, and public speaking. He is best known for his book *How to Win Friends and Influence People*.

Carr, Michael J., 1952-. US editor, writer, and translator with some 500 book title credits, including over fifteen *New York Times*, *Wall Street Journal*, and *Los Angeles Times* best sellers.

Carrey, Jim, 1962-. Canadian-US actor, comedian, screenwriter, and film producer. Carrey has performed in over forty feature films.

Carter-Scott, Chérie, 1949-. US author, speaker, and life coach. Carter-Scott is known for her book *If Life Is a Game, These Are the Rules*.

Cass, Moses Henry, 1927-. Australian statesman (member of the House of Representatives), and honorary fellow at the University of Melbourne.

Charlton, Jack, 1935-. English former footballer and manager. Charlton played on the team that won the 1966 World Cup. He won Manager of the Year during his first season with Middlesbrough (19734).

Clark, Frank A., 1911-1991. US author and cartoonist. Clark ministered to tens of thousands of people via his newspaper cartoons. He is known as the creator of *The Country Parson* sermons, which were published by some 200 newspapers.

Clason, George S., 1874-1957. US author, businessman, and soldier. Clason served in the US army during the Spanish-American war. He is known for his book *The Richest Man in Babylon*.

Clinton, Bill, 1946-. US politician who served as the forty-second president of the United States (19932001). He attended Oxford as a Rhodes Scholar.

Clinton, Hillary, 1947-. US politician who served as secretary of state under President Barack Obama. She attended Yale Law School, where she received a doctorate of law degree in 1973.

Collier, Robert, 1885-1950. US author of self-help and New Thought metaphysical books. Collier is known for his book *The Secret of the Ages*.

Confucius, 551-479 BC. Chinese teacher, politician, and philosopher. He is traditionally credited as the author and editor of classic Chinese texts, including the *Five Classics* (*Classic of Poetry, Book of Documents, Book of Rites, Book of Changes, Spring and Autumn Annals*).

Covey, Stephen R., 1932-2012. US author, businessman, educator, and speaker. He is best known for his book *The Seven Habits of Highly Effective People*.

Cowper, William, 1731-1800. English poet and hymnist. Cowper is regarded by some as one of the great modern poets. One of his poems, *The Negro's Complaint*, was often quoted by Martin Luther King Jr.

Craik, Dinah M., 1826-87. English novelist and poet. She is principally remembered for her novel *John Halifax, Gentleman.*

Darwin, Charles, 1809-82. English naturalist and geologist. Darwin is known for his groundbreaking contribution to evolutionary theory. Many consider his book *On the Origin of Species* the foundation of evolutionary biology.

De Beauvoir, Simone, 1908-86. French writer, philosopher, feminist, and political activist. Beauvoir is known for her treatise *The Second Sex* and her novels *She Came to Stay* and *The Mandarins.*

De Botton, Alain, 1969-. Swiss-born, British-based philosopher, writer, and television presenter. Botton has published over ten books, including *How Proust Can Change Your Life.* He is cofounder of The School of Life.

De Montaigne, Michel, 153-392. French essayist and philosopher. Montaigne's essays influenced other notable figures including Francis Bacon, René Descartes, Blaise Pascal, Jean-Jacques Rousseau, and Shakespeare.

DeJoria, John Paul, 1944-. US businessman and philanthropist. DeJoria is cofounder of John Paul Mitchell Systems (one of the largest privately held companies in the United States) and the Patrón Spirits Company.

Diderot, Denis, 1713-84. French philosopher, art critic, and writer. Diderot was a prominent figure during the Enlightenment, and cofounder, chief editor, and contributor to *L'Encyclopédie.*

Disney, Walt, 1901-66. US entrepreneur, cartoonist, animator, voice actor, and film producer. Disney was cofounder of the Walt Disney Company.

Drucker, Peter F., 1909-2005. Austrian-born US management consultant, author, and educator. Drucker was regarded by many as the founder of modern management.

Durant, Will, 1885-1981. US author, historian, and philosopher. Durant is known for *The Story of Civilization*, an eleven-volume series completed over forty years in collaboration with his wife, Ariel Durant. The Durants won the Pulitzer Prize for General Nonfiction (1968) and the Presidential Medal of Freedom (1977).

Edison, Thomas, 1847-1931. US inventor and businessman. His hundreds of inventions include the phonograph, the motion picture camera, and the incandescent lightbulb.

Einstein, Albert, 1879-1955. German-born theoretical physicist. He developed the general theory of relativity. Along with quantum mechanics, it is one of the two pillars of modern physics.

Eisenhower, Dwight D., 1890-1969. Thirty-fourth president of the United States. A five-star general, he served as supreme commander of the Allied Forces in Europe during World War II.

Emerson, Ralph Waldo, 1803-82. US essayist, lecturer, and poet. A champion of individualism and a leader of the Transcendentalist movement, he published dozens of essays and delivered over 1,500 public lectures across the United States.

Erasmus, Desiderius, 1466-1536. Dutch Renaissance humanist, Catholic priest, social critic, teacher, and theologian. His bronze statue erected in 1622 in Rotterdam, the city of his birth, is the one of the oldest in the Netherlands.

Escalante, Jaime, 1930-2010. Bolivian-born US educator. Escalante is known for teaching calculus at Garfield High School, East Los Angeles, during 1974-91. He was the subject of the 1988 film *Stand and Deliver*.

Federation of All Young Buddhist Associations of Japan. A federation of Buddhist groups, the earliest dating back to 1898, created to preserve Buddhist-based culture.

Ferrazzi, Keith, 1966-. US author. Ferrazzi is the founder and CEO of the research institute and strategic consulting firm Ferrazzi Greenlight. He is known for his books *Never Eat Alone* and *Who's Got Your Back*.

Foch, Ferdinand, 1851-1929. French soldier and military theorist, Allied commander-in-chief during World War I. Foch was made a British field marshal in 1919 and marshal of Poland in 1923 and received additional awards from many other nations.

Ford, Henry, 1863-1947. US industrialist, founder of the Ford Motor Company. He revolutionized transportation in American by providing an automobile that the middle class could afford.

Frank, Anne, 1929-45. German-born diarist. Frank's wartime diary, *The Diary of a Young Girl*, has been the basis of several plays and films and is one of the world's most widely known books.

Galbraith, John K., 1908-2006. Canadian-born US economist, author, and diplomat. Galbraith's most famous work is his trilogy on economics: *American Capitalism, The Affluent Society*, and *The New Industrial State*.

Galilei, Galileo, 1564-1642. Italian astronomer, physicist, engineer, philosopher, and mathematician. Galileo played a major role in the scientific revolution during the Renaissance. He is regarded by some as the father of observational astronomy and modern physics.

Gandhi, Arun, 1934-. Indian-American sociopolitical activist. Grandson of Mohandas Gandhi, he founded the M. K. Gandhi Institute for Nonviolence, dedicated to applying the principles of nonviolence locally and globally.

Gates, Bill, 1955-. US tech pioneer, businessman, and philanthropist. Cofounder of Microsoft. In 2015, Forbes ranked him as the richest person in the world. Gates has signed the Giving Pledge, meaning that he plans to give most of his net worth to philanthropic causes during his life or upon his death.

Gautama, Siddhártha, ca. 520-440 BC. The sage on whose teachings Buddhism is founded, he is regarded as the "Supreme Buddha." His teachings were passed down orally for some 400 years before being committed to writing.

Gerrold, David, 1944-. US science fiction screenwriter and novelist. Gerrold is known for his novelette *The Martian Child*, which won both Hugo and Nebula awards and was adapted into a 2007 film.

Grove, Andy, 1936-. Hungarian-Born US businessman, engineer, and author. Former CEO of Intel Corporation, he is a pioneer in the semiconductor industry.

Guest, Edgar A., 1881-1959. Prolific English-born US poet. Guest penned some 11,000 poems during his lifetime.

Hardy, Darren, 1971-. US author, speaker, and publisher of *SUCCESS* magazine. Hardy's books include *The Entrepreneur Roller Coaster* and *The Compound Effect*.

Harris, Sydney J., 1917-86. US journalist, drama critic, teacher, and lecturer. Harris wrote eleven books and received rewards from the American Civil Liberties Union and the Chicago Newspaper Guild.

Haskins, Henry S., 1875-1957. Stockbroker and aphorist. Haskins's writings were edited and published anonymously in 1940 under the title *Meditations in Wall Street*.

Henley, William, 1849-1903. Poet and critic. Nelson Mandela credits his poem "Invictus" as helping him during his incarceration at Robben Island.

Hepburn, Katharine, 1907-2003. US actress and Oscar winner known for her fierce independence and spirited personality. The American Film Institute named Hepburn the greatest female star of classic Hollywood cinema.

Hill, Napoleon, 1883-1970. US author. Hill was one of the earliest authors of personal-success literature. His best-selling book *Think and Grow Rich* is the most famous in the genre.

Hoffer, Eric, 1898-1983. US philosopher. Hoffer wrote ten books, including *The True Believer*, and received the Presidential Medal of Freedom in 1983.

Holmes, Chet, 1957-2012. US author, adviser, businessman. Holmes has advised over sixty Fortune 500 companies. Charlie Munger called him "America's greatest sales and marketing executive." He is known for his book *The Ultimate Sales Machine*.

Holmes, Oliver Wendell, 1809-94. US physician, poet, professor, lecturer, and author. Holmes was widely regarded as one of the best writers of his day. He is known for his Breakfast-Table series, beginning with *The Autocrat of the Breakfast-Table*.

Huffington, Arianna, 1950-. Greek-born US author and columnist. Cofounder and editor in chief of the *Huffington Post*, she has written some ten books.

Huxley, Thomas, 1825-95. English biologist. Huxley is known as "Darwin's Bulldog" for his advocacy of Charles Darwin's theory of evolution. He received the Royal, Wollaston, Clarke, Copley, and Linnean medals.

Hyatt, Michael, 1955-. US author, speaker, and former chairman and CEO of Thomas Nelson Publishers. Hyatt has written eight books, including *Platform: Get Noticed in a Noisy World*.

Jackson, Curtis, 1975-. US rapper, actor, entrepreneur, and media producer. Jackson is better known as "50 Cent."

Jobs, Steve, 1955-2011. US tech entrepreneur, visionary, and inventor. Cofounder of Apple, he is known for revolutionizing personal computers, animated movies, music, telephones, tablet computing, and digital publishing. Jobs is one of the greatest business leaders of all time.

Johnson, Lyndon B., 1908-73. Thirty-sixth president of the United States, who pushed through the landmark Civil Rights Act of 1964, outlawing discrimination based on race, color, religion, six, or national origin. Johnson's presidency marked the peak of modern liberalism in the United States after the New Deal era.

Jones, James Breckenridge, 1918-80. US author and businessman, founder of Abundavita. He mentored James Earl Shoaff, who mentored Jim Rohn, who mentored Tony Robbins and other influential figures in the personal development arena.

Jordan, Michael, 1963-. US professional basketball player and businessman. A two-time inductee into the Basketball Hall of Fame, he is regarded by some as the greatest basketball player of all time.

Kasparov, Garry, 1963-. Russian (formerly Soviet) chess grand master, writer, and political activist. Kasparov became the youngest-ever undisputed world chess champion in 1985, at age 22. Some regard him as the greatest chess player of all time.

Keller, Helen, 1880-1968. US author, political activist, and lecturer. Though both deaf and blind, Keller wrote thousands of letters and traveled the world to improve the lives of the physically handicapped.

Kennedy, John F., 1917-63. Thirty-fifth president of the United States, JFK is the youngest-ever elected president. He was assassinated in November 1963 by Lee Harvey Oswald.

Kipling, Rudyard, 1865-1936. English short-story writer, poet, and novelist. During the late nineteenth and early twentieth centuries, Kipling was one of the most popular writers in the UK, in both prose and verse. His works include the novel *Kim*, the collection of short stories in *The Jungle Book*, and the poem "If—." Kipling received the Nobel Prize in Literature in 1907.

Lamb, Karen, -. Australian author and lecturer at the Australian Catholic University. Author of five books, Lamb is known for her biography *Thea Astley: Inventing Her Own Weather*.

Lao Tzu, ca. 550-450 BC. Chinese philosopher and poet, reputed founder of Taoism, author of the *Tao Te Ching*. His name is an honorific title meaning "Old Teacher," or "Old Man."

Lincoln, Abraham, 1809-65. Sixteenth President of the United States. After rising from humble beginnings, Lincoln led the United States through the Civil War and spearheaded the abolition of slavery in the United States. He is regarded as one of America's greatest heroes.

Lombardi, Vince, 1913-70. US football player, coach, and executive. Head coach of the Green Bay Packers football team during the 1960s, he is considered one of the greatest coaches in professional football history. The NFL's Super Bowl trophy is named in his honor.

Machiavelli, Niccolò, 1469-1527. Italian Renaissance historian, politician, diplomat, philosopher, humanist, and writer. Machiavelli is best known for his book *The Prince*. He is regarded by many as the founder of modern political science.

Maltz, Maxwell, 1889-1975. US cosmetic surgeon and author. His book *Psycho-Cybernetics*, published in 1960, continues to be a popular self-help book today. Maltz believed that self-image is the cornerstone of all the changes that take place in a person.

Mandela, Nelson, 1918-2013. South African antiapartheid activist, politician, and philanthropist. Convicted by the South African government of conspiracy to overthrow the state, he served 27 years in prison. After his release, he went on to become the first black president of South Africa. Mandela received the 1993 Nobel Peace Prize.

Maxwell, John C., 1947-. US speaker, pastor, and author of over seventy books. Three of his books have sold over a million copies each. He speaks to Fortune 500 companies and international government leaders. Maxwell's books and talks focus primarily on leadership.

Megginson, Leon C., 1921-2010. US professor of management and marketing at Louisiana State University. A prolific author, he served as president of the Southwestern Social Science Association and the Southern Management Association.

Meridius, Maximus Decimus. Fictional Roman general played by Russel Crowe in Ridley Scott's 2000 film *Gladiator*. Meridius resembles the historical figures Narcissus, Spartacus, Cincinnatus, and Marcus Nonius Macrinus.

Merton, Thomas, 1915-68. US writer, mystic, poet, social activist, and student of comparative religion. Merton wrote over seventy books, mostly on spirituality and social justice. He is known for his autobiography *The Seven Storey Mountain*.

Michelangelo, 1475-1564. Italian sculptor, painter, architect, and poet. Considered one of the greatest artists of all time, he is known for his *Pietà*, *David*, and the Sistine Chapel ceiling painting.

Montapert, Alfred A., 1906-1997. US author and philosopher. He is best known for his book *The Supreme Philosophy of Man: The Laws of Life*.

Morley, J. Kenfield, -. US businessman. President of the Advitagraph Corporation, which produced advertising motion pictures and manufactured projectors.

Mourkogiannis, Nikos, -. Founder of Nikos & Company, a "purpose led strategic restructuring company." He is an adviser to CEOs of top companies around the world.

Parton, Dolly, 1946-. US singer, songwriter, actress, author, businesswomen, and humanitarian. Parton is one of the most honored female country performers of all time, with twenty-five gold, platinum, and multi-platinum albums. She was inducted into the Country Music Hall of Fame in 1999.

Pascal, Blaise, 1623-62. French mathematician, physicist, inventor, writer, and philosopher. Pascal developed Pascal's Wager, Pascal's Triangle, Pascal's Law, and Pascal's Theorem, concerning God, binomial coefficients, fluid mechanics, and projective geometry, respectively. He is known for his book *Pensées* (Thoughts).

Pausch, Randy, 1960-2008. US professor of computer science, human-computer interaction, and design at Carnegie Mellon University, Pennsylvania. Pausch was diagnosed with terminal pancreatic cancer in 2006. After learning that he had three to six months to live, he gave a lecture titled *The Last Lecture: Really Achieving Your Childhood Dreams*. He then cowrote the book *The Last Lecture*, which became a *New York Times* best seller.

Peck, M. Scott, 1936-2005. US psychiatrist and author of over fifteen books. His first and best-known book, *The Road Less Traveled*, has sold over ten million copies.

Peters, Tom, 1942-. US writer on business management practices. He is best known for the book *In Search of Excellence*, which he cowrote with Robert H. Waterman Jr.

Poehler, Amy, 1971-. US actress, comedian, voice artist, director, producer, and writer. Poehler is known as a cast member on the NBC television series *Saturday Night Live*. In 2011, she was included on *TIME* magazine's "100 Most Influential People in the World."

Quillen, Robert, 1887-1948. US journalist and humorist. Quillen's work has appeared in hundreds of newspapers in the United States, Canada, and the UK.

Rand, Ayn, 1905-82. Russian-born US novelist, philosopher, playwright, and screenwriter. Rand is known for her novels *The Fountainhead* and *Atlas Shrugged*. She is the developer of a philosophical system which she called Objectivism.

Robbins, Tony, 1960-. US motivational speaker, personal finance instructor, self-help author, and executive coach. Robbins is known for his books *Unlimited Power*, *Unleash the Power Within*, and *Awaken the Giant Within*.

Robinson, Ken, 1950-. English author, speaker, and international adviser on education. Robinson is known for his book *The Element: How Finding Your Passion Changes Everything*. His 2006 TED talk "Do schools kill creativity?" has been watched over 37 million times.

Rohn, Jim, 1930-2009. US entrepreneur, author, and motivational speaker. Rohn's books and audio recordings have influenced millions of lives (including mine). Tony Robbins, Mark Victor Hansen, Jack Canfield, and Brian Tracy all credit Rohn with influencing their lives and careers.

Russell, Bertrand, 1872-1970. British philosopher, logician, mathematician, historian, writer, social critic, and political activist. Russell is a founder of analytic philosophy. His philosophical essay "On Denoting" is regarded by many as a paradigm of philosophy. Russel cowrote *Principia Mathematica*, a three-volume work on the foundations of mathematics.

Sagan, Carl, 1934-96. US astronomer, cosmologist, astrophysicist, astrobiologist, and author. Sagan assembled the first physical messages that were sent into space (the Pioneer plaque and the Voyager Golden Record). He narrated and cowrote the popular 1980s television series *Cosmos: A Personal Voyage*.

Saint Augustine, 354-430. Christian theologian and philosopher. Augustine is viewed as one of the most important church fathers in Western Christianity. *The City of God* and *Confessions* are among his greatest works.

Samit, Jay, 1961-. US entrepreneur, digital media innovator, and author. Samit is CEO of SeaChange International and has held senior positions at Universal Studios, EMI Recorded Music, and Sony. Samit's first book, *Disrupt You! Master Personal Transformation, Seize Opportunity, and Thrive in the Era of Endless Innovation*, has become a best seller.

Sandberg, Sheryl, 1969-. US technology executive, activist, and author. Sandberg became the COO of Facebook in 2008, and the first woman to serve on Facebook's board, in 2012. She cowrote *Lean In: Women, Work, and the Will to Lead*.

Selassie, Haile, 1892-1975. Ethiopian regent 1916-30. Emperor of Ethiopia 1930-74. Within the Rastafari movement, Selassie is revered as the returned messiah of the Bible—God incarnate. He is a defining figure in Ethiopian and African history.

Seneca, 4 BC-AD 65. Roman Stoic philosopher, statesman, and dramatist. Seneca wrote 124 philosophical letters and 9 tragedies. He was first a tutor and then an adviser to the emperor Nero. Following a plot to kill Nero (in which Seneca was likely uninvolved), Nero ordered him to kill himself, which he did.

Shakespeare, William, 1564-1616. English poet, playwright, and actor. Shakespeare is widely regarded as the greatest writer, and the greatest poet, in the English language. His plays have been translated into every major living language and are regularly performed today, 400 years after his death.

Sher, Barbara, 1943-. US speaker, career and life coach, lecturer, author. Sher lectures at Fortune 100 companies, professional conferences, and at universities all over the world. Her books have sold millions of copies.

Socrates, 470-399 BC. Greek philosopher credited as one of the founders of Western thought. Socrates is known chiefly through the accounts of other writers, including his students Plato and Xenophon, and the plays of his contemporary Aristophanes. Found guilty of impiety and corrupting the minds of Athenian youth, he was put to death with a potion of poison hemlock.

Sullivan, Louis H., 1856-1924. US architect. Regarded as the "father of skyscrapers," he was the second architect in history to be posthumously awarded the AIA Gold Medal (the American Institute of Architects' highest award) in 1944.

Thiel, Peter, 1967-. US entrepreneur, venture capitalist, hedge fund manager, and social critic. Former CEO and cofounder of PayPal, and chairman and cofounder of Palantir, he was Facebook's first outside investor. Thiel concentrates his philanthropic efforts on what he calls "potential breakthrough technologies."

Thompson, Hunter S., 1937-2005. US journalist and author. Thompson became internationally known with his book *Hell's Angels*. As research, he spent a year living and riding with "the Angels." Thompson also wrote the popular novel *Fear and Loathing in Las Vegas*.

Tolstoy, Leo, 1828-1910. Russian writer. Regarded as one of the greatest novelists of all time, he is best known for *War and Peace* and *Anna Karenina*. His book *The Kingdom of God Is Within You* is said to have profoundly influenced Mohandas Gandhi and Martin Luther King Jr.

Tracy, Brian, 1944-. US motivational speaker and author, chairman and CEO of Brian Tracy International, a company specializing in training and development of individuals and organizations. He has consulted for over 1,000 companies and spoken to more than five million people. He has written over seventy books.

Truman, Harry S., 1884-1972. Thirty-third president of the United States. Truman helped found the United Nations and helped create the $13 billion ($130 billion in 2015 dollar value) Marshall Plan to rebuild Western Europe.

Twain, Mark, 1835-1910. US author and humorist. Twain is known for his novels *The Adventures of Tom Sawyer* and *The Adventures of Huckleberry Finn*. He is regarded by some as the "father of American literature."

Tyson, Mike, 1966-. US boxer. Tyson won his first nineteen professional bouts by knockout, twelve of them in the first round. At age 20, he became the undisputed world heavyweight champion. Tyson has been inducted into the World Boxing Hall of Fame.

Waitley, Denis, 1933-. US motivational speaker, writer, and consultant known for his audio series *The Psychology of Winning* and his books *Seeds of Greatness* and *The Winner's Edge*. Waitley has been inducted into the International Speakers' Hall of Fame.

Walton, Sam, 1918-92. US businessman and entrepreneur, founder of Wal-Mart and Sam's Club. He was included in *TIME* magazine's list of the "100 Most Influential People of the 20th Century."

Watts, Alan, 1915-73. British-born US philosopher, writer, and speaker. Watts was a renowned interpreter of Eastern philosophy for a Western audience.

Welch, Jack, 1935-. US former business executive, author, and chemical engineer, chairman and CEO of General Electric 1981-2001. In 2005, he published *Winning*, a book on management. The book reached number 1 on both the *New York Times* and *Wall Street Journal* best-seller lists.

Widener, Squire Bill, 1840-1920. US teacher. Widener was a Confederate soldier and a prominent community figure, justice of the peace, and spiritual adviser.

Wilde, Oscar, 1854-1900. Irish playwright, novelist, essayist, and poet. One of London's most popular playwrights during the early 1890s, he wrote *The Picture of Dorian Gray*, *The Soul of Man under Socialism*, *Lady Windermere's Fan*, and *An Ideal Husband*. His masterpiece is perhaps *The Importance of Being Earnest*.

Williamson, Marianne, 1952-. US spiritual teacher, author, and lecturer. Williamson has published ten books, including four *New York Times* number 1. best sellers. She has been a guest on popular television programs such as *The Oprah Winfrey Show* and *Larry King Live*.

Winfrey, Oprah, 1954-. US media mogul, talk show host, actress, producer, and philanthropist, best known for *The Oprah Winfrey Show*. She was awarded the Presidential Medal of Freedom in 2013.

Ziglar, Zig, 1926-2012. US author, salesman, and motivational speaker. Ziglar has written fourteen books on success. His first book, *See You at the Top*, was rejected by some thirty publishers before going on to become one of his most successful books.

Sources

Each quote in this book was chosen for its message. Great care was taken to ensure correct attribution. Most quotes have been verified using either the original source or another reputable source. But in some instances, this was not possible. The author apologizes for any misquote or misattribution.

The Foundation: Accept Full Responsibility for Your Life

Dale Carnegie, from *Be of Good Cheer*, by Marvin J. Ashton, 1987.

Anne Frank, from *The Stolen Legacy of Anne Frank*, by Ralph Melnick, 1997.

Leo Tolstoy, from *Words of Wisdom to Live By*, by Alfred A. Montapert, 1986.

Napoleon Hill, from *Think and Grow Rich*, by Napoleon Hill, 1937.

Jack Welch, from *Winning*, by Jack Welch, 2005.

Katharine Hepburn, from *Words of Wisdom*, by William Safire and Leonard Safir, 1990.

The Dean and Howard Roark, from *The Fountainhead*, by Ayn Rand, 1943.

William Henley, from "Invictus," in *A Book of Verses*, by William Henley, 1888.

Ken Robinson, from *The Element*, by Ken Robinson, 2009.

Ralph Waldo Emerson, from *It's Up to Us*, by John Graham, 1999.

Hunter S. Thompson, from *The Proud Highway*, by Hunter S. Thompson, 1997.

Jaime Escalante, from *It's All in the Frijoles*, by Yolanda Nava, 2000.

Alain de Botton, from *The Consolations of Philosophy*, by Alain de Botton, 2001.

Peter Thiel, from *Zero to One*, by Peter Thiel, 2014.

Lao Tzu, from *Hua Hu Ching: Teachings of Lao Tzu*, by Brian Browne Walker, 1992.

Harry S. Truman, from *American Presidents, Religion, and Israel*, by Paul Charles Merkley, 2004.

Jim Rohn, from Jim Rohn's works, *The Art of Exceptional Living*, *The Power of Ambition*, or *The Day that Turns Your Life Around*, 1994, 1994, 2003, respectively.

Stephen R. Covey, from *The Educator's Book of Quotes*, by John Blaydes, 2003.

Oliver Wendell Holmes, from The *Professor at the Breakfast-Table*, by Oliver Wendell Holmes, 1860.

Hillary Clinton, from *Living History*, by Hillary Clinton, 2004.

Frank A. Clark, from *An Analysis of Supervisor Conflict Management Style and Subordinate Satisfaction with the Performance Appraisal Interview*, by Mary Ellen Kelly, 1993.

Pillar 1: Perceive the World to Your Advantage

Albert Einstein, from *The New Quotable Einstein*, by Alice Calaprice, 2005.

Blaise Pascal, from *The Thoughts of Blaise Pascal*, translated from the text of M. Auguste Molinier, by C. Kegan Paul, 1901.

Oprah Winfrey, from "Oprah Winfrey's 20 Best Inspirational Quotes," on www.her.yourstory.com, article by Tanvi Dubey, Jan. 30, 2015.

Siddhārtha Gautama, the Buddha, from the *Dvedhavitakka Sutta*, translated from the *Pāli* by Thanissaro Bhikkhu, 1997.

David Gerrold, from *A Matter for Men*, by David Gerrold, 1989.

Ken Robinson, from *The Element*, by Ken Robinson, 2009.

Bertrand Russell, from *The History of Western Philosophy*, by Bertrand Russell, 1945.

J. Kenfield Morley. Evidence for attribution is unclear, referencing Quote Investigator (www.quoteinvestigator.com): "the earliest evidence found by QI for this type of saying appeared in French in a book by Alphonse Karr who declined to give an ascription."

William Shakespeare, from *Hamlet*, by William Shakespeare, 1603.

Arianna Huffington, from *Thrive*, by Arianna Huffington, 2014.

Walt Disney, from *The Story of Walt Disney*, by Diane Disney Miller, as told to Pete Martin, 1957.

Tony Robbins, from "Tony Robbins Quotes—His 75 Most Motivational Lines," on www.selfmadesuccess.com, article by Justin Bryant (publication date unknown), accessed Feb. 2016.

Jay Samit, from *Disrupt You!*, by Jay Samit, 2015.

Richard Bach, from *Illusions*, by Richard Bach, 1977.

Desiderius Erasmus, from *Collectanea Adagiorum*, by Desiderius Erasmus, 1500.

Sydney J. Harris, from *On the Contrary*, by Sydney J. Harris, 1964.

Steve Jobs, from *Steve Jobs: Visionary Entrepreneur*, an interview with Steve Jobs by Silicon Valley Historical Association, 1994.

Thomas Carlyle, from *Chartism*, by Thomas Carlyle, 1840.

Ken Robinson, from *The Element*, by Ken Robinson, 2009.

Marianne Williamson, from *A Return to Love*, by Marianne Williamson, 1992.

Jay Samit, from *Disrupt You!*, by Jay Samit, 2015.

Michel de Montaigne, from *The Essays of Michel de Montaigne*, by Michel de Montaigne, Book III, 1580.

Helen Keller, from *The Story of My Life*, by Helen Keller, 2009.

Peter Thiel, from *Zero to One*, by Peter Thiel, 2014.

Oscar Wilde, from *An Ideal Husband*, by Oscar Wilde, 1895.

Pillar 2: Always Strive for Growth

Oscar Wilde, from *The Picture of Dorian Gray*, by Oscar Wilde, 1890.

Jim Rohn, from Jim Rohn's works, *The Art of Exceptional Living*, *The Power of Ambition*, or *The Day that Turns Your Life Around*, 1994, 1994, 2003, respectively.

Warren Buffett, quoted during a Q&A session at Berkshire Hathaway's Annual Meeting of 2008.

Socrates, from *Apology*, by Plato, ca. 390 BC.

Nelson Mandela, from *The Work of the Ministerial Staff*, by James H. Hudson, 2003.

Oscar Wilde, from *The Soul of Man under Socialism*, by Oscar Wilde, 1891.

Unknown. A variant on Voltaire's phrase "the best is the enemy of the good."

Tom Peters, quoted by Jim Rohn in *Leading an Inspired Life*, by Jim Rohn, 2011.

George Gordon Byron, from *Epitaph to a Dog*, by George Gordon Byron, 1808.

Socrates, from *Republic*, by Plato, ca. 390 BC.

Jim Rohn, from Jim Rohn's works, *The Art of Exceptional Living*, *The Power of Ambition*, or *The Day that Turns Your Life Around*, 1994, 1994, 2003, respectively.

Alan Watts, from *The Tao of Philosophy*, edited transcripts of Alan Watts by Mark Watts, 1995.

Thomas Merton, from *The Wisdom of Desert*, by Thomas Merton, 1970.

Confucius, from *The Greatest Minds and Ideas of All Time*, by Will Durant, compiled and edited by John R. Little, 1996.

Will Durant, from *The Greatest Minds and Ideas of All Time*, by Will Durant, compiled and edited by John R. Little, 1996.

Seneca, from *Moral letters to Lucilius*, by Seneca, translated by Richard Mott Gummere, 1917.

Bill Clinton, quoted during his statement before signing the American Competitiveness in the Twenty-First Century Act and Non-Immigrant Worker Fee Legislation, 2000.

Unknown. Often attributed to Albert Einstein but with no substantive evidence found to support the attribution.

Galileo Galilei, from *Edge-tools of Speech*, by Maturin Murray Ballou, 1899.

John F. Kennedy, quoted during his address to the Massachusetts State Legislature, Jan. 9, 1961.

Edmund Burke, from *Reflections on the Revolution in France*, by Edmund Burke, 1790.

Darren Hardy, from *The Compound Effect*, by Darren Hardy, 2010.

John C. Maxwell, from "Is Your Environment Holding You Back?" on www.johnmaxwell.com, article by John C. Maxwell, July 10, 2014.

Denis Diderot, from Vol. 25, p. 667 of *L'Encyclopédie*, 1751-66.

Pillar 3: Set Your Goals, Then Plan and Execute

Tony Robbins, from *Awaken the Giant Within*, by Tony Robbins, 1992.

James Allen, from *As a Man Thinketh*, by James Allen, 1902.

Randy Pausch, from *The Last Lecture*, by Randy Pausch and Jeffrey Zaslow, 2008.

Alan Watts, original work unclear. Audio recording available online, titled "What if Money Was No Object?"

Ferdinand Foch, from *The 32d Infantry Division: World War II*, by Harold Whittle Blakeley, 1956.

Michelangelo, from *The Element*, by Ken Robinson, 2009.

Richard Branson, from @richardbranson on Twitter, 11:25 a.m., Apr. 9, 2012.

Will Durant, from *The Greatest Minds and Ideas of All Time*, by Will Durant, compiled and edited by John R. Little, 1996.

Dwight D. Eisenhower, from *Six Crises*, by Richard Nixon, 1962.

Darren Hardy, from *The Compound Effect*, by Darren Hardy, 2010.

Garry Kasparov, from *How Life Imitates Chess*, by Garry Kasparov, 2007.

Andy Grove, from *High Output Management*, by Andy Grove, 1983.

Jack Welch, from *Winning*, by Jack Welch and Suzy Welch, 2005.

Peter F. Drucker, from *The Definitive Drucker*, by Elizabeth Edersheim, 2006.

Simone de Beauvoir, from *The Ethics of Ambiguity*, by Simone de Beauvoir, 1947.

Francis Bacon, from *Essays*, by Francis Bacon, 1597.

Louis H. Sullivan, first read before the Architectural League of America, Toronto, 1902, published in *Kindergarten Chats and Other Writings*, by Louis H. Sullivan, 1947.

Robert Collier, from *The Secret of the Ages*, by Robert Collier, 1926.

Edgar A. Guest, from "It Couldn't Be Done," in *Collected Verse of Edgar A. Guest*, by Edgar A. Guest, 1934.

John Paul DeJoria, from "Business Tips from Once Homeless Billionaire, John Paul DeJoria," on www.forbes.com, article by Steven Bertoni, Oct. 28, 2013.

Joseph Addison, from *The Guardian*, no. 117 (newspaper founded by Addison's friend Richard Steele) July 25, 1713.

Will Durant, from *The Story of Philosophy*, by Will Durant, 1926.

Darren Hardy, from *The Compound Effect*, by Darren Hardy, 2010.

Mike Tyson, from "Everyone Has a Plan until They've Been Hit" (boxing adage), on www.barrypopik.com, article by Barry Popik, May 5, 2012.

Jim Rohn, from Jim Rohn's works, *The Art of Exceptional Living*, *The Power of Ambition*, or *The Day that Turns Your Life Around*, 1994, 1994, 2003, respectively.

Pillar 4: Understand "Success" and "Failure"

Curtis Jackson ("50 Cent"), quoted during his interview with Louis Gannon for *Live* magazine, from *The Mail on Sunday*, Oct. 25, 2009.

Andrew Carnegie, from *Miscellaneous Writings of Andrew Carnegie*, edited by Burton J. Hendrick, 1933.

Leo Tolstoy, from *What Then Must We Do?*, by Leo Tolstoy, 1886.

Squire Bill Widener, from *Theodore Roosevelt, an Autobiography*, by Theodore Roosevelt, 1913.

James Breckenridge Jones, from *The Laws of Success and The Abundavita Story!*, DVD published by Ron Henley International, 2013.

Rudyard Kipling, from "If—" by Rudyard Kipling, 1895.

Brian Tracy, from *The Psychology of Selling*, by Brian Tracy, 1988.

Jack Charlton, from *Reflections on Success*, by Martyn Lewis, 1997.

Oprah Winfrey, from *O, The Oprah Magazine*, Jan. 2003.

Thomas Edison, from *An Enemy Called Average*, by John L. Mason, 1990. (Note: Saying was in circulation while Edison was still alive, but substantive evidence for his attribution is lacking. Henry Dodd, or another, may be the originator.)

Chet Holmes, from *The Ultimate Sales Machine*, by Chet Holmes, 2007.

Andrew Carnegie, from *Autobiography of Andrew Carnegie*, by Andrew Carnegie and John Charles Van Dyke, 1920.

Henry Ford, from Vol. 25 of Advanced Management: Quarterly Journal, 1958.

Oscar Wilde, from *The Thorny Paradise*, by Edward Blishen, 1975.

Bernard M. Baruch, from *A Philosophy for Our Time*, by Bernard M. Baruch, 1954.

Zig Ziglar, from www.ziglar.com, Aug. 30, 2015.

Unknown. Often attributed to either Winston Churchill or Abraham Lincoln, but with no substantive evidence found to support the attributions. A close match is found in

How to Say a Few Words, by David Guy Powers, 1953; the quote is ascribed "anonymous."

Michael Jordan, from *Nike Culture*, by Robert Goldman and Stephen Papson, 1998.

Bill Gates, from *The Words of Power*, by George Antwi, 2012. (While the original source could not be found, this quote is widely attributed to Gates.)

Abraham Lincoln, from *The Success Journey*, by John C. Maxwell, 1997. (While the original source could not be found, this quote is widely attributed to Lincoln.)

Napoleon Hill, from *Think and Grow Rich*, by Napoleon Hill, 1937.

Pillar 5: Embrace Change and Take Risks

Karen Lamb, from *The Addison-Wesley Science Handbook*, by Gordon J. Coleman and David Dewar, 1997.

Eric Hoffer, from *The Passionate State of Mind, and Other Aphorisms*, by Eric Hoffer, 1955.

John K. Galbraith, from *Economics, Peace and Laughter*, by John K. Galbraith, 1971.

Sheryl Sandberg, from *Lean In*, by Sheryl Sandberg, 2013.

Sam Walton, from *Made in America*, by Sam Walton, 1992.

Leon C. Megginson, quoted during the presidential address delivered at the Southwestern Social Science Association convention in San Antonio, Texas, Apr. 12, 1963.

Jim Rohn, from Jim Rohn's works, *The Art of Exceptional Living*, *The Power of Ambition*, or *The Day that Turns Your Life Around*, 1994, 1994, 2003, respectively.

Arun Gandhi, from *Arun Gandhi Shares the Mahatma's Message*, by Michael W. Potts, 2002.

Niccolò Machiavelli, from *The Prince*, by Niccolò Machiavelli, 1532.

Maxwell Maltz, from *Psycho-Cybernetics*, by Maxwell Maltz, 1960.

Brooks Atkinson, from *The Complete Art of Public Speaking*, by

Jacob Morton Braude, 1970 (corroborated in a number of other publications, including *Public Papers of the Presidents of the United States: Jimmy Carter*, 1981.)

Robert Quillen, from "Editorial Epigrams" in *The Evening Repository* (newspaper published in Canton, Ohio), March 27, 1924.

Leo Buscaglia, from *Living, Loving & Learning*, by Leo Buscaglia, 1982.

Amy Poehler, quoted during the Harvard University Class Day Commencement Address, May 26, 2011.

Keith Ferrazzi, from *Never Eat Alone*, by Keith Ferrazzi and Tahl Raz, 2005.

Barbara Sher, from *I Could Do Anything if I Only Knew What It Was*, by Barbara Sher, 1994.

H. Jackson Brown Jr., from *P.S. I Love You*, by H. Jackson Brown Jr., 1990. (Note that H. Jackson Brown Jr. credits this to his mother.)

Denis Waitley, from *The Winner's Edge*, by Denis Waitley, 1980.

Jim Carrey, quoted during the Maharishi University of Management Commencement Address, May 2014.

Alfred A. Montapert, from *Inspiration & Motivation*, by Alfred A. Montapert, 1982.

Arianna Huffington, from "A Conversation between Arianna and Her Daughters," on www.huffingtonpost.com, blog post by Arianna Huffington, Nov. 17, 2011.

Nelson Mandela, from *Long Walk to Freedom*, by Nelson Mandela, 1995.

Steve Jobs, quoted during the Stanford University Commencement address, June 12, 2005.

William Cowper, from *Poems by William Cowper of the Inner Temple, Esq. in Two Volumes: Vol. 1*, by William Cowper, 1800.

Pillar 6: Work Well with Others and Strive Toward Leadership

Lyndon B. Johnson, from *Public Papers of the Presidents of the United States: Lyndon B. Johnson*, 1967.

Andrew Carnegie, from *Developing the Leader Within You*, by John C. Maxwell, 1993.

Carl Sagan, from *Pale Blue Dot: A Vision of the Human Future in Space*, by Carl Sagan, 1994.

Dale Carnegie, from *How to Win Friends and Influence People*, by Dale Carnegie, 1936.

Michel de Montaigne, from *The Essays of Michel de Montaigne*, by Michel de Montaigne, Book I, 1580.

Alain de Botton, from *The Consolations of Philosophy*, by Alain de Botton, 2001.

Henry Ford, Bill Ford quoting his great-grandfather (Henry Ford) during the Q4 2005 Ford Motor Company Earnings Conference Call, Jan. 2006.

Unknown. The author found this quote among his personal notes, but could not reliably ascribe a source.

Peter Thiel, from *Zero to One*, by Peter Thiel, 2014.

Jim Rohn, from Jim Rohn's works, *The Art of Exceptional Living*, *The Power of Ambition*, or *The Day that Turns Your Life Around*, 1994, 1994, 2003, respectively.

Ralph Waldo Emerson, from *Self-Reliance*, by Ralph Waldo Emerson, 1841.

Seneca, from *The Consolations of Philosophy*, by Alain de Botton, 2001.

Mark Twain, quoted in a letter to George Bainton, Oct. 15, 1888, from *The Art of Authorship*, by George Bainton, 1890.

Dale Carnegie, from *How to Win Friends and Influence People*, by Dale Carnegie, 1936.

Michael Hyatt, from "What I learned at Tony Robbins' Business Mastery Event," on www.michaelhyatt.com, article by Michael Hyatt, Jan. 17, 2014.

Unknown, from *Hearts on Fire*, by Joji Valli, 2014. (Valli ascribes the quote to an unknown priest.)

Aristotle, from Book II, 1109 a27, of *Nicomachean Ethics*, by Aristotle, ca. 350 BC.

Zig Ziglar, from *Secrets of Closing the Sale*, by Zig Ziglar, 1984.

Jay Samit, from *Disrupt You!*, by Jay Samit, 2015.

Federation of All Young Buddhist Associations of Japan, from *The Teaching of Buddha*, by the Federation of All Young Buddhist Associations of Japan, 1934.

Vince Lombardi, from "Famous Quotes by Vince Lombardi," on www.vincelombardi.com, publication date unknown, accessed Feb. 2016.

Jim Rohn, from Jim Rohn's works, *The Art of Exceptional Living*, *The Power of Ambition*, or *The Day that Turns Your Life Around*, 1994, 1994, 2003, respectively.

Haile Selassie, from *Speeches Delivered on Various Occasions*, by Haile Selassie, 1960.

Chérie Carter-Scott, from *The Differences Between Management and Leadership*, by Chérie Carter-Scott, 1994.

Peter F. Drucker, from *The Daily Drucker*, by Peter F. Drucker and Joseph A. Maciariello, 2004.

John K. Galbraith, from *The Age of Uncertainty*, by John K. Galbraith, 1977.

Dolly Parton, from *The Most Important Things I Know*, by Lorne Adrian. 1997.

Pillar 7: See the Big Picture

Nelson Mandela, from *Long Walk to Freedom*, by Nelson Mandela, 1995.

Alain de Botton, from *The Consolations of Philosophy*, by Alain de Botton, 2001.

George S. Clason, from *The Richest Man in Babylon*, by George S. Clason, 1926.

Unknown. Some attributions to Fidel Castro exist, but with no substantive evidence found to support the attribution.

Alain de Botton, from *The Consolations of Philosophy*, by Alain de Botton, 2001.

Arianna Huffington, from *Thrive*, by Arianna Huffington, 2014.

Charles Darwin, from *The Autobiography of Charles Darwin*, by Charles Darwin, 1887.

Maximus Decimus Meridius, fictional character played by Russell Crowe in *Gladiator*, directed by Ridley Scott, story by David Franzoni, 2000.

M. Scott Peck, from *The Road Less Traveled*, by M. Scott Peck, 1978.

Marcus Aurelius, from *The Emperor's Handbook: A New Translation of The Meditations*, by C. Scot Hicks and David Hicks, 2002.

Shannon L. Alder, from *Write Your Legacy*, by Richard Campbell and Cheryl Svensson, 2015. (Confirmed by Shannon L. Alder.)

Steve Jobs, from "What's Next?: Steve Jobs's Vision, So on Target at Apple, Now Is Falling Short," in the *Wall Street Journal*, article by G. Pascal Zachary and Ken Yamada, May 25, 1993. (Note that earlier versions of similar quotes exist, the earliest being Ed Wynn as quoted in "Ed Wynn Doesn't Yearn to Be Wealthiest Man in Cemetery," in the *Boston Globe*, Jan. 19, 1932.)

Bertrand Russell, from *Uncertain Paths to Freedom*, papers by Bertrand Russell, edited by Richard A. Rempel and Beryl Haslam, 2000.

Michael J. Carr, quoted during e-mail correspondence between Michael J. Carr and James Melouney.

Will Durant, from *The Greatest Minds and Ideas of All Time*, by Will Durant, compiled and edited by John R. Little, 1996.

Moses Henry Cass, quoted during a speech on environmental
   policy at the Ministerial Meeting of the OECD Environment
   Committee in Paris, delivered Nov. 13, 1974, from *Australian
   Government Digest*, Vol. 2, no. 4, 1974.

Unknown. Often attributed to the Dalai Lama, but with no substantive evidence found to support the attribution. Possibly
   derived from "An Interview with God . . ." on www.apple-
   seeds.org. Author unknown, publication date unknown,
   accessed Feb. 2016.

Nikos Mourkogiannis, from *Purpose: The Starting Point of Great
   Companies*, by Nikos Mourkogiannis, 2006.

Thomas Huxley, from Vol. 2 of *Life and Letters of Thomas Henry
   Huxley*, by his son Leonard Huxley, 1903.

Henry S. Haskins, from *Meditations in Wall Street*, by Henry S.
   Haskins, 1940.

Dinah M. Craik, from *A Woman's Thoughts about Women*, by
   Dinah Craik, 1858.

Saint Augustine, from *The Confessions of Saint Augustine*, by Saint
   Augustine, written ca. 400, published by Hendrickson, 2004.

Recommended Reading

1. Mortimer Adler, *How to Read a Book* (also, Adler's recommended reading list)
2. Jim Rohn, *The Day that Turns Your Life Around*
3. Napoleon Hill, *Think and Grow Rich*
4. Darren Hardy, *The Compound Effect*
5. Mihaly Csikszentmihalyi, *Flow*
6. Marcus Aurelius, *Meditations*
7. Eckharte Tolle, *A New Earth*
8. Will Durant and Ariel Durant, *The Lessons of History*
9. William Safire, *Lend Me Your Ears*
10. The Arbinger Institute, *Leadership and Self-Deception*
11. Stephen R. Covey, *The 7 Habits of Highly Effective People*
12. Peter F. Drucker, *The Effective Executive*
13. Jay Samit, *Disrupt You!*
14. Sam Walton, *Made in America*
15. George Clason, *The Richest Man in Babylon*

ACKNOWLEDGMENTS

This book would not exist without a great many people. But even before family, friends, editors, designers, typesetters, and others made their invaluable contributions, there came a thought: to write a book worthy of giving to my younger self and to my future children. How that thought came, I don't know. Why it came, I can only guess. But *that* it came is something I will be eternally grateful for.

To my parents, thank you for laying a solid foundation for my life: a foundation mixed with elements from each of the eight parts of this book. "Fortunate" is too weak a word.

To my family and friends, thank you for your feedback on early drafts, "final" revisions, and long lists of titles and subtitles. More importantly, thank you for being so tolerant and supportive while I dedicated so much time to this endeavor—especially you, Peter. Writing a book takes a toll, not just on the author but also on those closest to them.

To my editor, Michael J. Carr, thank you for your impeccably diligent editing. Not only did you elevate this book to a new level, you gave me a master class in writing. It would be my pleasure to work with you again, should I be so privileged.

Finally, my deepest thanks to each exemplar quoted in this book. Your words have inspired me, and it is my hope that through this book, your words will continue to inspire others.

About the Author

James Melouney spends a lot of his time thinking, writing, and speaking about life and success. For many years, he has been exploring why some people live wildly successful lives while others only trudge along, merely existing.

James was born in South Africa, has lived and worked in Canada and the United States, and currently resides in Sydney, Australia. With a background in finance and management consulting, he delivers talks to senior corporate executives, government officials, and university audiences.

When he's not writing or crafting business strategy, James is probably surfing the Australian east coast or heading to the mountains in search of the next powder day.

CPSIA information can be obtained
at www.ICGtesting.com
Printed in the USA
LVOW03s1239140917
548672LV00001B/1/P